I0075069

THE PHILO SYSTEM
OF
PROGRESSIVE POULTRY KEEPING

BY E. W. PHILO

****

The purchasers of this book are given the right to make and use any and all appliances herein contained. Owners of the book may employ others to make the appliances; but persons who do not own the book have no right to use the appliances nor the System.

****

First published in 1907

****

Reprinted by
New York History Review
in 2022

The Philo System of Progressive Poultry Keeping
by E. W. Philo, 1907
Reprinted by New York History Review

ISBN: 978-1-950822-27-0

Printed in the United States of America

The Philo Poultry Institute building still stands at 1575 Lake Street in Elmira, New York.

INTRODUCTION.

In publishing our system of Progressive Poultry Keeping we simply give the facts about all branches of the work that have been learned from experiments conducted by the hand of the writer. We have learned by actual tests that many theories advanced by the majority of poultry writers are without foundation. Men gifted with the power of imagination and the ability to write an entertaining article have been given too much space in publications.

Our experience in poultry keeping dates back over a period of thirty-five years, and the mistakes made during that time if, properly explained, would fill a book much larger than this one. While many of our mistakes were expensive and discouraging, we were determined to win out, and as the failures came, we had the opportunity to study the causes, and again start from the foundation to overcome the difficulties. Many times the discoveries were surprising to us, as they will, no doubt, be to you, and were not put down as facts until each of them had been tested for at least five years, and many of them much longer.

We have learned that artificial heat supplied to chickens is not only unnecessary, but better poultry may be raised without it. The average ordinary heated wood brooder is too complicated and expensive, and there is too much danger of chilling, overheating, or burning the chickens. When they come into this world they are supplied with an abundance of heat and all we have to do is to retain it.

When green cut bone is fed liberally to breeding stock, good eggs from which to hatch strong chickens are not obtained, neither are the eggs likely to be fertile.

The best two pound broilers can be raised when confined to a space of one square foot, when there are not too many in the flock.

Pullets may be properly matured in a space of one and a half square feet, and a laying hen will do her best when given three square feet of space. While it is generally understood that the largest egg yields from laying hens are obtained from the smallest flocks, the system is not in general use.

It is not uncommon to get six eggs from six hens in a flock, seven consecutive days. To get sixty eggs from sixty hens in a flock, one day in a year is hardly possible, and, as far as our knowledge goes, is not on record. Sixty hens properly bred and kept in ten colony coops will lay sixty eggs per day many days in the year, and at least twenty-five per cent. more eggs than the flock containing sixty hens. When chicks do their best they must also be kept in small flocks.

The natural desire of men to get rich quick without much knowledge of the business, or capital to invest is probably the excuse for large flocks. They estimate the profits from a given number of hens they wish to keep, and figure that the cost of the poultry plant would be less when the fowls are maintained in large flocks.

Our aim has not been simply to get the greatest returns, as we have given more thought to economy and simplicity in labor saving devices, making it possible to keep large numbers of laying hens in small flocks at no greater expenditure for appliances than where large numbers are kept together. Everything in connection with our system is made with a view of using all kinds of material to the best advantage, and without waste. The lumber, wire, muslin, and waterproof covering required in the construction of our appliances are all standard sizes and may readily be obtained in all villages and cities.

While the advantages of the Philo System are many they can all be summed up in one word, "success". Follow the entire plan as outlined and success is sure.

Very truly yours,
E. W. PHILO.

STARTING IN THE POULTRY BUSINESS.

The best way to start in the poultry business is to begin with two pairs of the best birds (not related) that you can afford to purchase. When the details of our system are carefully followed and the breeding stock is right, it will be perfectly safe to handle as large a business from the start as you can provide necessary appliances for and the time required for proper attention and care. However, the disadvantage is likely to be inferior stock that possibly has been inbred, or that has not been raised in a way to build up a constitution of vigor and hardiness which is the foundation to a successful business.

By starting with two pairs of the best stock obtainable, with the assurance that they have not been inbred, you will get large profits more quickly than to start with a dozen or more birds. It would not be difficult to raise twenty-five pullets and a number of cockerels the first season from two hens, furnishing breeders that would give you three hundred pullets the second year, and this would enable you to do as large a business as you like the third season. While these figures may look large, they are not over estimated, as we are getting still greater returns right here in our own yard, and are not giving them as careful attention as it is possible to do.

Purchasing the best eggs obtainable for hatching is also a desirable way to start in the business, and in many cases would be less expensive than to buy the stock. We would not advise you to buy stock that would cost less than ten dollars per pair, unless you know positively the quality and can get them for less money; and it would be still better to pay twenty-five dollars each, provided you could get birds so well bred as to be worth the money.

Two sittings of eggs at five dollars each should produce more and better stock than you could purchase for an equal amount of money, and it sometimes happens that better birds are raised from eggs bought than from those raised by the producer. If you can find eggs from very choice stock for ten dollars a sitting, it would prove a good investment. In other words, if you can get either stock or eggs that are really worth the money, almost any price is not too much to pay, as what you raise from them would soon bring you large additional returns.

If you are to buy eggs for the foundation stock they should be hatched in February or March provided the fertility is guaranteed. If not, get the eggs during the natural season for hatching, April, May or June.

E. W. Philo

The advantages of getting eggs for hatching that are laid during January or February are that you are sure they were laid by winter layers; and after breeding in this manner for two or or three generations your hens will lay as naturally through the cold winter months as others do in June.

If they are to be hatched during the winter or early spring, one of the brooder coops should be ready when they hatch, which will provide the necessary protection to keep them in the best possible condition at all times.

Before eggs are ordered, some provision should be made for hatching them as you cannot afford to take chances on finding a broody hen, or on the prompt delivery of an incubator. The successful man is the one who is just a little in advance of his business, and takes time by the forelock.

LOCATION.

One of the advantages of our system is that you can start in the business where you now live, provided you have four square feet of land for each fowl you wish to keep. Three-fourths of the lands is for fowls, and one-fourth for walks. It is better, however, to have twice the amount of land required, that you may alternate the poultry yard with the garden, thereby purifying the ground and making a garden that will astonish the natives.

Should the soil be low and damp it will be necessary to fill in with sand or gravel so it will be slightly above the ground around it. If dry, and there is some gravel in the soil, it will not be necessary to fill in. Stony or coarse lumpy soil should be avoided, as it is necessary to keep the ground mellow, which is easily accomplished by spading, with the aid of the hens to keep it stirred up.

In selecting a new location to make a specialty of the poultry business you will find it of advantage to get a place where the soil is composed principally of sand or gravel. It is also an advantage to have it slightly rolling with a South or East exposure to the sun. By selecting a gravelly soil the hens are furnished a natural grit which is not only a saving in the expense account of the plant, but is actually preferred by the fowls to the manufactured grit.

A nice apple orchard is a fine place during the hot summer months, and the increased production of the trees, and the improved qual'ty of the fruit will add much to the profits of the plant. Grape vines and plum trees grow quickly and make a desirable shade, as well as being very productive.

The combination of poultry, fruit, and garden is one of the best, and the possibilities from an acre lot can hardly be estimated.

To make the combination complete a few colonies of bees should be kept. There is hardly a thing that the writer has undertaken that has brought as large returns for the amount of capital invested and labor required as the honey bee. One season 200 pounds of white clover honey in one pound boxes were taken from one colony of bees, made up from two new swarms combined. The time required to care for the bees was less than a day and the value of the honey was thirty dollars. This of course was an uncommon yield, still half that amount is not an uncommon yield, and the returns are large enough to make the business interesting.

SELECTING BREEDERS TO PRODUCE LAYERS.

It would be treading upon dangerous ground to mention any one breed of fowls as being superior to others as egg producers. In our experience it is not so much the breed as the strain, as careful and intelligent breeding will do wonders in a few generations. It will make sitters of non-sitters, and non-sitters of the breed that is often found broody, if you wish to breed to that end. It is also possible to make the very best layers from poor ones, and very poor ones from the best.

We have selected the Single Comb White Orpingtons simply for the reason that there is more money in them for us at the present time than in many of the other breeds. After carefully selecting and breeding them for seven years we find they will lay more eggs in a year than any fowls we ever kept, although we consider it possible to make as good layers from many of the older breeds. Like all breeds, they have their good qualities, but we will not go into the details of any particular breed, as it is largely a matter of choice of the poultryman.

When undertaking the fancy part of the poultry business, there are advantages in selecting a new breed, and growing up with it. There are many noted breeders of the older varieties, making it difficult to compete with them, while in the newer varieties there are less experts at the work, making it possible to gain a substantial footing at an eariler date.

For utility breeding, either eggs or meat, it would be exceedingly difficult to improve on many of the old standbys.

The systems for selecting layers that are now advertised in the poultry journals were practiced by the writer fifteen years ago. The width of the hen and general make-up will determine to a certain extent her value as a layer. It is not always true with us as we find some of the hens that are not quite as wide behind as the widest, are superior layers, and the only correct way is to know to a certanity how many eggs each individual hen will lay in a given time, but we do not consider it necessary to have a complete year's record, as every hen will show her productiveness in each lot of eggs laid between her rest periods. After a hen has laid a certain number of eggs she will either rest for a few days or become broody when the stock of egg-making material has been exhausted. The time required for this rest seldom varies, it generally being just one week from the time the last egg was laid before furnishing the first one of the new lot. This is, of course, when the hens are properly fed and in good condition.

In our tests we find the number of eggs laid between the rest periods are sometimes not over nine, while others will lay forty to fifty or more without stopping. The number of eggs laid between each rest is not sure to indicate the value of the hen as an egg producer, as it often happens that the hen producing twelve eggs between the rest periods, will lay them in twelve consecutive days, while the one laying more eggs without stopping, often requires two days to lay one egg. A day and date record for two months should determine the quality of the hen as an egg producer.

The pullets that first begin laying, or those that commence while quite young are generally the best layers. The philosophy of this is that the pullets that lay first have matured most quickly because constitutionally more vigorous. The same physical conditions will enable them to produce a larger number of eggs than the pullet that was slower in coming to maturity because of a less vigorous constitution.

In selecting layers there are two points to be considered that we have never known to fail. The largest individual hens of any breed are never the best layers, and the hens laying the largest eggs never lay as many of them in a given length of time. When finding a hen that will lay twelve eggs in twelve consecutive days, the eggs will seldom weigh over twenty-five ounces to the dozen, and the hen laying very large ones requires two days to make every egg. As long as eggs are sold by the dozen it is an advantage to the poultryman to breed hens that will lay eggs averaging about twenty-five ounces to the dozen. They are not considered small, and will sell at the highest market price.

The color of the eggs is also another point to be considered, as eggs of a uniform color, either white or brown, are more attractive and will generally bring a little better price when marketed.

Breeding from the best layers for three or four generations will produce a strain of fowls that is capable of producing its like, while a good laying hen that has not the breeding back of her is not likely to produce her equal.

In summing up we will give a few points that go to make up the most productive hen.

One that is not over large for her breed, and that is especially wide and deep in her fluff.

One that has a very large crop for her size and has it well filled at night, and one that lays eggs of a medium size.

SELECTING BREEDERS FOR BROILERS.

In selecting breeders for broilers, capons, etc., one's aim should be extreme hardiness, early maturity and large, well developed frames. These qualities are all possible with the best layers, still these best layers may not be the best for the broiler farm. The hen that lays only every other day puts more vitality into the egg.

She is generally the largest of her breed, and her eggs also are large, furnishing more nutriment for the growing embryo and more yolk for the chick to absorb, to give it a good start in life after being hatched.

With the average stock, first crosses will make the best broilers, and make them more quickly than the ones raised from thoroughbreds. This is on account of the breeders not being related, and is the point which should convince poultrymen that the practice of inbreeding is a mistake. It is possible, however, to get as good results from the thoroughbred stock when they have not been inbred and when their constitution and vigor have been retained to the highest degree.

The "First Cross" is breeding together two distinct breeds and the offspring would be hybrids, not valuable to use as breeders, for mating together, nor for crossing with a thoroughbred of another breed.

SELECTING BREEDERS FOR EXHIBITION.

In breeding for exhibition, the American Standard of Perfection should be consulted, and birds selected conforming as nearly as possible to the Standard requirements. When it is possible, the males should be especially strong in the points where the females are weakest. The size and shape of the hen, and the color of the male bird are reproduced in nine cases out of ten. A Black Minorca male crossed with Barred Rock females will produce black fowls shaped like Rocks, and a Rock male crossed with Minorca hens will produce barred fowls shaped like Minorcas. While there may be exceptions to the rule, it may safely be relied upon in nearly every case. The chicks hatched from the first six eggs laid after the mating, are not as likely to follow the color of the male as those laid after the first six.

Leg bands should be used on all breeders and a careful record kept; giving as many details as possible, including weight, color, etc., just as given on a score card as indicated on another page, the necessary cuts being made after carefully comparing the bird with the illustration in the Standard and making the cuts for imperfections as indicated therein.

For pedigree breeding this record is indispensable, as the only means by which we can ascertain facts about breeders of the past, that we may know to a certainty the true qualities of the stock from which our birds have sprung. It is also an educator in itself, as it plainly shows from one generation to the next the improvements made, and how they were brought about; besides, the stock thus raised has a market value greatly in excess of stock of the same quality that has been produced by chance or haphazard breeding.

There are sixteen individual toe marks that may be made by punching the webs between the toes in all combinations. As soon as the chicks are hatched they should be thus marked, and a careful record kept showing their ancestors. When the chicks have matured it is an easy matter to tell the breeders which are producing valuable show birds, and these should be retained for many years, or as long as they will produce superior stock.

It sometimes happens that the best specimens do not produce the best stock. Several years ago we lost all of our best male birds of one breed at the close of the hatching season. There was one bird left that we considered worthless as a breeder. We were anxious to raise a few more chickens, and it was too late in the season to purchase a valuable bird, so we concluded to make a trial of the one we had. To our surprise the best specimens we raised that season were from this male bird which we had considered worthless, and the chickens were especially strong in points in which the old bird was weak. The breeding back of this bird was of the very best, and the qualities produced by him were the superior qualities of his ancestors.

Official Score Card of the American Poultry Association

Date........................	Variety......................
Owner......................	Sex........................
Address....................	Band No....................
Entry No...................	Weight......................

	SHAPE	COLOR	REMARKS
Symmetry...........	......	......	....
Weight or Size.......	......	......	....
Condition..........	......	......	....
Head and Beak......	......	......	....
Eyes..............	......	......	....
Comb.............	......	......	....
Wattles and Ear-lobes..	......	......	....
Neck.............	......	......	....
Wings............	......	......	....
Back.............	......	......	....
Tail..............	......	......	....
Breast............	......	......	....
Body and Fluff......	......	......	....
Legs and Toes.......	......	......	....
*Hardness of Feather..	......	......	....
†Crest and Beard.....	......	......	....

*Applies to Games and Game Bantams
†Applies to Crested breeds

Name of Judge ______________________________

Secretary ______________________________

This form should be used to keep an accurate record of the breeding stock. We can furnish printed books, as above, of a hundred sheets for 25 cents, postpaid.

Seconds from carefully bred stock are more valuable for breeding purposes than the firsts from stock that has been carelessly bred.

THE BEST AGE FOR BREEDERS.

In this matter our experience differs from the theories advanced by most breeders, as it is generally claimed that the cockerels mated to two year old hens are best.

We get best results from breeders both male and female that are just past one year old. The pullets having then reached maturity, the time of laying large eggs, are then fully developed and should be in better physical condition than either earlier or later in life.

A male bird that has been with hens constantly for a year is not likely to be a good breeder during the succeeding winter, and needs a few months' rest. You will be surer of satisfactory results by using a younger bird just matured.

Our breeding stock is all hatched in February or March and is grown as rapidly as possible, commencing to lay in August or September, and laying from sixty to one hundred eggs each before the new year, when they are to be used as breeders.

From twenty-five to fifty per cent. of the winter-hatched pullets will go through the molt in October or November, generally completing it in about half the time required by old hens. After completing the molt they are full-fledged hens and in prime condition for breeders or the show room. The fertility of the eggs is then at its best, and the chicks after being hatched, are more easily raised than those from old or very young hens, besides reaching maturity at an earlier age.

This system also has the advantage of raising stock that comes to laying during the cold Winter months as naturally as the average stock lays in May and June

When raising exhibition fowls, it is best to use your choice breeding stock as long at they will produce birds of superior quality. Females from five to ten years old are often valuable.

FERTILITY.

Three days after mating, fertile eggs may be expected. If the matings have been changed, some results from the former mating will be in evidence. The following six eggs are also likely to produce birds showing the characteristics of either mating.

Careful tests have shown that not over twelve eggs will be fertilized after the sexes have been separated, and in many instances the fertility ends with the sixth egg. After two weeks' mating we may expect nothing but the results from the last mating.

When a hen becomes broody she may be taken from one pen and placed in another where she should again commence laying in one week. The first egg laid will be fertilized by the last mating.

FERTILITY AND HATCHABILITY

A very large per cent. of all poultry keepers are now learning that fertile eggs and those capable of producing strong chickens are two different things. Every egg from a hen or pen of fowls may be strongly fertilized, yet not composed of the proper material to furnish a chick. It should not be difficult to find the reason for the defect, still hundreds of people are puzzled, and think the trouble is due to improper incubation. In ninety-nine out of one hundred cases the trouble is in the feeding, and the food used is too fattening and lacks bulk.

A pen of fowls purchased from a party who had paid but little attention to their feeding may serve as an illustration. The first eggs laid after they came to us were fertile, but the chicks died in the shell at about the tenth day. The next lot did better, but did not hatch. However, after these hens had been fed on coarse, bulky food, including clover, for about three weeks, their eggs hatched well, and have done so ever since. The progress made in their improvement along this line has been steady and before the close of the season we expect to produce chickens which will leave the shell with a bound, and grow from a tiny ball to a mature hen in the shortest required space of time.

For the benefit of those having trouble along this line we will say that the foods used to overcome these defects in eggs from which to hatch strong chickens are as follows: Whole oats wheat bran, sweet milk, lean beef, and green food, either cut clover or alfalfa, or sprouted oats.

In Summer we use a mash composed of at least three-fourths green food in some form, clover, alfalfa or lawn clippings,

BREEDING IN LINE.

Line breeding is to use our own stock and not to introduce new blood without the knowledge of what it will produce.

Inbreeding is generally practiced to start line breeding, although it is not the proper way for the best results, especially when breeding utility stock, as the vitality is weakened to a certain extent, requiring several years to overcome the bad effects.

Our way to start line breeding is to get eggs or stock from two poultrymen who are separated by as many miles as possible. The birds are not as likely to be related as those from the nearby poultry yards; and should they be related, the fact that they have been bred under different conditions of climate, etc., will render them of nearly as much value as birds not related. You will then carry two distinct strains and may use the male birds from one side to cross with the females of the other side. After the first cross it will be necessary to cross first cousins, which is not considered inbreeding, and this will produce stock that is more likely to inherit the good qualities of its ancestors.

CARE OF BREEDING STOCK.

Natural conditions are the essential points to success. While it is not possible in a cold climate, during the best breeding season of the year, to bring about perfectly natural conditions, we are to do so as nearly as possible.

It is necessary to commence the work before the first cold weather, that the change may be gradual and the fowls hardened under natural conditions to the extreme cold weather. They must be protected from the wind and direct draft, having at the same time the full outside weather conditions, and without being in the rain or snow. Our combined Summer and Winter Colony coop is well adapted to get the desired conditions. Other buildings that will answer the purpose, and save the cost of the colony coop, may easily be arranged with but little expense and labor.

We used the loft of an old barn for some of our best breeding stock one winter with very satisfactory results. There were no glass or window openings, so large openings were made on the south side six inches from the floor, six inches from the roof and six feet long, and the opening covered with muslin. A tight box three feet wide, three feet deep and just long enough to accomodate the fowls on two perches, allowing two feet in length for every five birds, was nailed in the rear of the room two feet above the floor, the opening of the box facing the south, or front of the room, and covered with a burlap curtain that was let down every night to retain the heat of the fowls, keeping them comfortable and at the same time supplying an abundance of fresh air. It was nearly as cold in the room outside of the roosting box as the outside weather conditions, yet the fowls in the box did not suffer, and their combs were not frosted.

Whole oats, dry wheat bran, cut clover and oyster shells were kept in boxes all the time, and a little wheat, buckwheat and barley was scattered in the litter at night after roosting time, so that in the morning they might exercise enough to warm up, and get their blood circulating. Cracked corn was used for the night food and scattered in the litter about three o'clock in the afternoon, which would keep them busy until roosting time. Water was given them in the morning and at noon; and on very cold days it was necessary to empty out the ice and furnish water four or five times during the day. If the water supply is allowed to run short the egg supply will suddenly be cut off.

We never feed condition powders, nor any of the patent material for promoting egg production, as it weakens the vitality of the stock and brings about unnatural conditions that are ruinous to a fertile egg supply. Green cut bone was never given, as we had discovered that eggs were not good for hatching after fowls were fed green cut bone during the winter. When lean beef can be had at a reasonable cost it is advisable to use it, and the results will be very satisfactory. Bone, if fed at all, should be dried and ground, or burned and crumbled. Grease, tallow and the marrow of the bones should never be fed except to fowls that are being fattened.

The pen of fourteen hens in the barn loft furnished us from eight to twelve and, occasionally fourteen eggs per day during the entire winter and spring. Nine eggs were set the 20th of January to test fertility, and nine chicks were the result. After the 20th, all perfect-shell eggs were incubated, and the lowest fertility during the Winter was five infertile eggs from one hundred. Several sittings showed one hundred per cent. fertility many times hatching every egg. The average hatch during the winter was over ninety per cent. from all eggs set, and ninety-eight per cent of the chickens assigned to our brooder coops were successfully raised.

KEEPING EGGS FOR HATCHING.

The very best treatment to give eggs for hatching is to set them the same day they are laid. When breeding from one or two hens this is not always advisable. They may be kept in good condition for a week or two, although we seldom incubate eggs over one week old. It is not uncommon to hatch eggs six weeks old, still it is not advisable, as it would be very difficult to raise the chickens. The loss of fertility is not the only thing to be taken into consideration. The evaporation of the moisture from the egg commences at once, taking with it some of the material necessary to grow a strong chicken, and making a depreciation in its value each succeeding day until the egg is worthless for incubation. The age of the egg before commencing to incubate has much to do with the amount of moisture to be supplied during the process of incubation. A perfectly fresh egg in a properly constructed incubator should never require supplied moisture. While the moisture may be supplied to bring out a satisfactory hatch the same quality of material cannot be replaced that was lost by evaporation, and the vitality of the chick is weakened to a degree corresponding to the age of the egg.

While keeping eggs for hatching it is not best to turn the eggs every day as is generally advised, for it weakens the albumen, making it more volatile and capable of penetrating the shell to a greater extent; besides bringing the germ capable of producing life nearer the surface of the shell, until finally it becomes attached, when it is worthless for incubation.

As the temperature is increased above the freezing point, evaporation increases in proportion. An egg kept at a temperature of eighty degrees will lose as much in weight in one week as it would in two weeks at a temperature of fifty-five degrees; and its value at two weeks is not equal to that of eggs kept at a temperature of fifty-five degrees, as the temperature is too high to retain the living germ in a perfectly dormant condition.

A low temperature does not weaken the vitality of the germ. If too low, it kills it outright and the egg may be kept as an infertile egg, and it will dry up in time without decaying. We have had good hatches from a basket of eggs where twenty-five per cent. of them were frozen and cracked open. About twenty-five per cent. of those not cracked were killed, while the other fifty per cent. produced fine chickens that were raised to maturity. and made healthy stock.

In all of our experiments the germ has been killed at some point below twenty-eight degrees above zero when exposed for at least twelve hours. A temperature below fifty degrees is better for eggs that are to be hatched than any point higher.

Eggs that are intended for incubation should never be placed with the small end down. It is not their natural position. After standing on the small end for a week or two the germ will

Three-pound White Orpington Roasters, Raised by The Philo System

18

The Philo System

float near the air cell in the large end of the egg. The chick will grow naturally for about ten days, then the growth will not be normal and the chick will not be properly matured at hatching time. It is also more likely to bring the chick's head at the small end of the egg, making it nearly impossible to free itself from the shell without help.

A temperature of eighty-five degrees for a few hours will start incubation, and the embryo will die during the next twenty-four hours, unless the temperature is raised to at least one hundred degrees. The egg will then decay.

A temperature of 115 degrees for five hours will kill the germ and the egg will appear infertile, and will keep nearly as long as an infertile egg.

CONTROLLING THE SEX.

To raise cockerels select a very strong, active male. A young bird is generally better than an old one. Then select hens that are from two to five years old. When but one hen is used in the breeding pen you will hatch from seventy to ninety per cent. cockerels. By increasing the number of females in the pen you will increase in proportion the number of females raised.

To raise nearly all pullets, use an old male bird or cockerel not especially active, mated to thirty or forty good lively pullets. You will not be likely to get the highest average fertility, but the chickens hatched will run largely to pullets. In one experiment we raised seventy pullets from seventy-seven chickens hatched.

The early hatched chickens are likely to run to cockerels to a much greater extent than those hatched from the same pens later in the season.

When the vitality of the male is greatly in excess of the females the chicks will run largely to males, and when the females are superior in that respect, a large portion of the chicks will be pullets.

SELECTING EGGS.

In selecting eggs from which to hatch our best layers, those weighing about twenty-five ounces to the dozen have the preference.

The shells should be smooth and uniform in shape and color. The ones that have a ridge around the center, and those with rough ends are rejected. When the rough end appears firm and the shell as thick as other portions of the egg it may safely be used.

Eggs having a metallic ring when being handled or rubbed between the hands are infertile, and the eggs that feel smooth and solid with a dull heavy ring like a ripe watermelon are best.

Large eggs are best to hatch broilers from as a rule, although the eggs weighing twenty-five ounces or more should produce quick maturing broilers.

Hens' eggs weighing more than thirty-two or less than twenty-four ounces to the dozen should never be set.

ARTIFICIAL INCUBATION.

The success of artificial incubation depends fully as much upon the quality and condition of the eggs as upon the machine or operator. Eggs produced under the conditions outlined in this book are easily hatched as compared with the eggs peoduced without any definite knowledge as to what is actually required.

But when the eggs are right, nine out of every ten failures are due directly to improper care the first week of incubation, although the chick will develop under improper handling, it will not hatch properly unless it has been properly developed by the end of the first week.

If there has been too much cooling, or the temperature has been low during the first seven days it is exceedingly difficult to get satisfactory results; the hatch is likely to be delayed and chicks hatched with crooked toes. When they have been properly handled the first week the chances are good for a good hatch even though they suffer from neglect during the later stages, and after two weeks of proper handling they will hatch when subjected to very harsh treatment.

After the first week, the temperature of the eggs may drop to fifty degrees for several hours, with no serious damage. Of course it is much better to keep the temperature within regular limits, but you need not be frightened because of variations, if not continued too long.

FIRST WEEK (102).

At the end of the first twenty-four hours after the eggs have been placed in the machine the thermometer should register about one hundred and two degrees with the bulb touching the upper surface of the egg. This temperature should be maintained as steadily as possible during the first week with but little airing.

The relative position of the eggs should be changed at least twice daily and three times is better when they can be quickly changed without much cooling. The machine should not be opened more than two minutes at a time during the first week.

In turning it is not important that the eggs should be turned exactly half way over, simply change their position.

Nature has provided for the very frail condition of the embryo during the first five days in two ways: First, by giving a hen the instinct to stick closely to the nest during this time, and secondly by allowing the embryo to float to the surface no matter what position the egg is in, during the first five days, that it may come in contact with the heating surface of the hen's body. After five days, when the embryo becomes stationary, there is quite a network of blood veins, and the rapid movement of the heart causes the blood to circulate more than half way around the egg, thereby generating heat that is a help in overcoming excessive cooling.

SECOND WEEK (103)

At the beginning of the second week the blood veins should completely encircle the egg near the air cell. Should there be a space not covered it would indicate a lack of heat, too much cooling, or a deficiency in the egg. If there is a clear space of a quarter of an inch between the extreme ends of the blood veins, and the egg is not at fault, the defective work of the first week may be partially overcome by carrying the temperature a half degree higher than is best under natural conditions during the remainder of the hatch.

When properly developed at the beginning of the second week, the temperature should be carried as nearly as possible at 103 degrees. The eggs should be turned two or three times daily as during the first week, and when turning the last time at night they should be cooled about five minutes when the room is from sixty to seventy degrees. If above seventy degrees they should be cooled one minute longer for every two degrees above seventy degrees. When the room temperature is below sixty, one minute should be taken from the five, for every five degrees cooler which would allow but one minute (about the time required to turn the eggs), in a room temperature of forty degrees. If the temperature of the eggs should be found above 103 degrees the eggs should be cooled five minutes longer for each degree too high. If found at 104 degrees they should be cooled ten minutes. or fifteen minutes if found at 105 degrees. If at any time the temperature should be at 106 or beyond, it may be quickly reduced by sprinkling the eggs with cold water.

Should the temperature of the eggs get below the desired point at any time do not cool them nor turn them; close the machine quickly and allow the eggs to warm up first. If the lamp should accidently go out, allowing the eggs to get cold, a few flat bottles or rubber bags of hot water, or cloths wrung out of hot water laid on the eggs will quickly restore the heat.

THIRD WEEK (103 1-2)

The rules as above for the second week are used during the last week, and the only changes made are to allow the temperature to run a half degree higher, and cool eggs five minutes longer, making the standard time for cooling ten minutes in place of five, and the temperature of the eggs 103½ degrees in place of 103.

By cooling the eggs the last thing at night they have a better chance to regain the lost heat, and are not likely to get overheated before morning.

On the seventh, twelfth and seventeenth days cool the eggs a full half-hour in a room temperature of about seventy degrees. In cooling the eggs thus, the contents contract, drawing through the pores of the egg shell a good supply of oxygen that is needed for the proper development of the chick.

The above directions apply to machines heated with hot air from above. When they are heated from the bottom or are heated with hot water, the temperature should be maintained one-half degree cooler than above.

Never under any conditions put eggs on top of the eggs on the trays so there will be two layers.

When the regulator of a machine has been properly adjusted, give it plenty of time to do its work before readjusting. Many hatches are ruined by playing with the regulator. After the eggs have been cooled the damper will sometimes open with a temperature of ninety degrees. When they are thoroughly heated through and before settling down to business the thermometer will register 104 or 105 degrees before it has time to reach the correct adjustment. The fact that the thermometer registers a little high does not indicate that the inside of the eggs has reached that degree of heat, as it requires several hours to change the temperature of the egg more than one degree.

While no absolute rule can be given as to what degree of heat will kill the germ, yet the following will serve as a guide in determining: A temperature of 108 degrees for ten hours the first week; of 110 for same time the second week; and of 115 the third week, will almost surely kill the germ, so that no chick can be hatched.

TESTING.

The eggs should be tested as soon as the germ can be detected, which is about five days for eggs with white shells, and one week for eggs with brown or dark colored shells. In testing hold the egg between the thumbs and fingers of both hands, keeping the hands as flat as possible to exclude the light near the egg. Close the hands on the egg so there will not be any openings for light between the hands and egg. Then by holding the egg before a strong light you can see perfectly the condition of the egg and its contents. Egg testers are not to be compared with this system after having a little practice and learning just how to hold the egg.

Three eggs may be tested in this manner in the same time required to test one with an ordinary tester. Testing is best done at night. Look through the side of the egg, not the end.

Discard all eggs that are perfectly clear, and those having a decided dark ring around the embryo, as these are imperfectly fertilized and will not produce chickens.

Chickens have more difficulty in getting out of the shells when the temperature has been carried too low than they do when the average temperature has been full high enough. Too much cooling the first week will retard the growth of the embryo to such an extent that the albumen will not all be consumed. The chick will hatch a day or two late and will be glued to everything it touches

Unless your machine is very poorly constructed, moisture should never be supplied before the last week, and then is not required when newly laid eggs are being incubated. When the hatch is delayed and the chicks are slow in breaking the shell, dampen a woolen cloth with hot water and lay it over the eggs.

As soon as the chicks are dried off they should be removed at once to the brooder. (See Brooding.)

HATCHING WITH HENS.

All sorts of interesting and uninteresting advice has been given about setting hens. When persons have one good hatch they take it for granted that they have solved the problem.

Regarding the location of the nest, the advice most generally given is to place it on the ground. After careful tests for thirty years we are not prepared to say that the ground is a better place to set a hen than the loft of a barn.

Poor results in hatching with the hens may be traced to but few causes, provided the eggs are what they should be. If eggs are accidentally broken in the nest, the shells of the other eggs must be thoroughly cleaned so that the pores may be opened for the admission of air to the growing chicks. During the first week of incubation it will not injure the embryo if the egg is coated with the contents of the broken egg for twenty-four hours, and then thoroughly cleaned. If coated twelve hours the second week the chances are against it, and if the egg remains entirely coated for two hours the third week the chick will die.

The quiet hen that would naturally be considered the best sitter is really the poorest hatcher, as she retains the same position on the nest too long at a time, not giving the eggs air or the embryo the exercise by moving about and changing the position of the eggs. The hens doing the best work are those having a nervous temperament, changing about on the nest and changing the position of the eggs in the nest with their beaks.

When you have a close sitter, she should be lifted every time you have the opportunity, changing the eggs about in the nest with your hands. The eggs that feel cool, or not quite as warm as others, should be placed in the center of the nest.

You can save every chick by removing the eggs as soon as the first one is found pipped, and placing them between wollen cloths thick enough to retain the heat and keeping them near the stove or in a temperature from eighty to ninety degrees. This would not answer for three or four eggs containing chicks without keeping them in a warmer place, but where there are ten or more the heat of the chicks will do the work when it is properly retained. Your chicks will then be free from lice and may be raised in our brooder without artificial heat.

We once shipped by express to a point three hundred miles away, eggs that were about to hatch. They were billed out eggs, and received as chickens with a one hundred per cent. hatch. The next week we received a letter from the party receiving the chicks saying that he had received a box containing fourteen fine chickens and some egg shells. These eggs had been properly incubated and would have hatched if they had been put on the floor and covered with a blanket, and kept warm.

A TRICK OF THE TRADE.

How to Save Fully Matured Chicks That Could Not Hatch Without Help.

At least one-third of all the chickens that are fully developed at the hatching time are unable to free themselves from the shell, and many times unable to make the first little opening. When they have been properly developed up to hatching time they can all be saved. In proportion to the number set there are just as many lost under hens as in incubators.

When the time has come for the egg to hatch, and there is no sign of life, hold the egg to the light and find the air cell. With a sharp-pointed knife-blade make an opening about the center of the air cell. By holding your thumb firmly against the side of the knife, near the point of the blade you will avoid cutting deep. Make the opening the size of a dime and you can then see the condition of the chick. If you find that its beak is through the inner lining of the egg, take a pin with the point upward and the head next the egg and, holding it at a right angle with the egg carefully chip out the shell around the large end of the egg commencing at the chick's beak. By being a little careful the shell may easily be chipped so it will disconnect the large end of the shell without injuring the membrane or causing it to bleed.

Then roll the egg up in a moistened strip of woolen cloth three inches wide by about ten inches long, the ends left open so the chick can get out without assistance and lay the egg back in the machine to hatch. Use hot water for moistening the cloth.

In the majority of cases it would not be necessary to break the shell loose with the pin as described, as the small opening in large end of the egg furnishes a liberal supply of air and the chicks that would not hatch otherwise come out nicely, without the danger of smothering just as they are about to leave the shell, as the woolen cloth causes the chick to sweat and softens the lining of the egg so the chick can make its escape without any great effort.

Our first experiment with the above plan was made several years ago after we had bought two sittings of expensive eggs.

When the time came for the eggs to hatch we found only ten eggs containing chickens, eight of these hatched out nicely but the other two could not crack the shell. The two eggs not hatched represented to us $4.20,—worth making an effort to save. We opened the large end and found the beaks open and the chickens gasping for breath in their effort to crack the shell. After watching them a few minutes their beaks closed, and the exhaustion caused by breathing was not so great. They were rolled up in cloth as above described and hatched out as bright and lively as the rest, and all of the ten chicks were raised to maturity.

WHY EXCESSIVE OR LIMITED MOISTURE INJURES THE HATCH.

We find many articles written on the moisture question. Reports from experimental stations, where elaborate tests have been made to ascertain the necessary amount of moisture to be furnished the egg during incubation in order to get the best results, fail to state the reasons why too much moisture or insufficient moisture would be injurious to a successful hatch.

In our experience we find that the more moisture retained in the eggs the better will be the chickens, and if it is necessary to supply moisture the chickens will not be as large, neither will they have as much strength as otherwise.

The amount of moisture retained or supplied to the eggs affects the size of the chicken, and when there is too much moisture, which is sometimes the case with sitting hens when on damp ground, the chickens will be too large for the egg and will be cramped for room, making it impossible for them to escape. They may sometimes have room enough to crack the shell, but this alone will not let the chickens out. After the shell is first cracked the chicken remains very quiet while absorbing the yolk, which requires from ten to twenty hours. Then it is necessary to make a complete turn in the egg, and by its efforts to turn, its beak is forced through the shell and when the complete circle has been made the end of the shell will be entirely cut off. When the chick is too large it is bound by its size, and cannot move around the regular course, so will smother or die in its efforts to move.

In many instances the chicken is too large to make the first small opening on account of not having room to move either legs or beak, for the movement of the legs, when there is room, causes a pressure on the shell by the beak which makes an opening.

While a very small chicken, or one incubated with excessive

evaporation of the eggs, is more likely to hatch than one that is too large, it very often happens that the chick lacks bulk, and, although it can make its turn in the egg and sometimes does so several times in an effort to find the way out, the shell will remain solid and the chicken will perish. It may kick and move around all it possibly can and yet be unable to bring the necessary pressure against the shell to make the first small opening.

Very large chickens and even those too large to make their escape are the best and can be raised with little effort as compared with those having been dwarfed by evaporation.

Judging by the letters coming into our office daily we think there will be over a million chickens saved during the season by applying "a trick of the trade." Many operators are saving from twenty to fifty chickens from each machine operated.

The dwarfed chickens are the ones more likely to have bowel trouble, although in nine cases out of ten the trouble is caused by the fact that the hens were not properly fed when producing the eggs, and the bowel trouble was hatched with the chickens.

BROODING THE CHICKS

Chickens may be raised and kept in perfect condition without supplying artifical heat.

After carefully testing our new brooder without artificial heat the old style brooder will be a thing of the past. (See Brooding without heat.)

But if for any reason you wish to use a heated brooder, the chickens, as soon as they are out of the shell, or at least a dozen or more of them, should be removed to the brooder having a temperature sufficient to keep them comfortable without crowding. It is not necessary to use a thermometer in the brooder, as it is better to watch the condition of the chickens and regulate the heat to make them comfortable. Many times when governing the heat of the brooder by fixed rules the chicks will be overheated or possibly chilled. Just a glance at them should tell one whether they are comfortable, and when guided in this manner the results will be more satisfactory.

Chicks removed to the brooder while very young learn the ways of the brooder more quickly than the ones that are left in the hatcher for a day or two.

The last efforts to free themselves from the shell is a greater tax on their systems than at any other time during incubation. Absorbing the yolk of the egg is the next to the last work accomplished by them before leaving the shell. By this act they are provided with food and should sleep quietly during the next twelve hours.

Large brooders are a mistake, no matter how many chickens are to be hatched or raised. It is better to keep them in small flocks, not over fifty the first week and twenty-five will do better than more. The second week they should be divided into flocks of twenty to twenty-five, and when forcing a few fine specimens for the show or some special work they should again be divided, leaving but ten in one brooder.

When there is much more room in the brooder than the chicks fill there is always circulating air that is a serious objection to the youngsters' welfare.

When artificial heat is used in the brooder it is just as important to have the heat automatically regulated as to regulate the temperature of the incubator.

THE FIRST FOOD.

After the chickens have been properly hatched, the success in raising them depends largely upon the care they get during the first week.

Nearly all writers say, "starve the chickens after they are hatched," some going as far as seventy-two hours before giving any food. That is not nature's way nor is it the best way. As soon as the chickens are old enough to run about and pick for food they should be given something nourishing to eat, and also something to drink.

It is generally claimed that if chickens are fed before they have digested the absorbed yolk of the egg, the food given will be used in place of the yolk, and the chicken will run down and finally die. The facts are, that when the yolk is not digested, it has been baked or hardened by improper incubation, especially over-heating leaving it in a hardened state causing it to become indigestible. Although the chicken will sometimes live six or eight weeks, it will dwindle and die in spite of all that can be done for it. The yolk must remain in a liquid form until it has been entirely used to build up the system of the chick. It matters not how much food has been given to the chicken, or how soon it was fed, the yolk will be used, if not rendered indigestible before being absorbed.

The first food should be bread crumbs slightly moistened with sweet milk. A very little at a time should be sprinkled around several times during the day where the chicks run, or about every two hours for best results. The bread used should be thoroughly baked and dried, so it will roll fine. Hard-boiled eggs rolled in the dry crumbs will add variety to the ration and help to give them a good start in life. Dry oatmeal or oat flakes should be given as soon as they will eat them, and should be fed once each day during the first three weeks. Both skim milk and water are placed before them as soon as they will drink. While it is possible to raise chickens without anything to drink during the first week, they do better when given both milk and water. After the first day they are given a very little Baby Chick Food twice daily, and the amount is increased each day until they are given all they will eat twice daily for the first three weeks, and longer if you can afford it. Dry coarse wheat bran is placed before them the first day, in little boxes about one inch deep and is kept before them constantly at all times, and at all ages of the poultry. When they are educated from the first to eat bran, it is astonishing to see the amount they will consume. If they are out of the bran for half a day and then given a fresh supply they will leave all other food and eat the bran. Half the bulk of food used for our poultry at all ages is dry wheat bran.

Fine grit, sand or fine gravel is given them from the first, although fed very sparingly the first day, or until the chickens know its value. If given all they will eat at first, they will sometimes eat too much, but are not so much inclined to do so when fed very young.

Finely cut clover is used for litter and a large portion of it is eaten by the chickens. It adds bulk to the food and helps to expand the crop, giving it a large capacity which is necessary to get the best results.

In feeding the sweet milk it is necessary to give it in a way that will prevent the chickens from getting it on them. We use the Cycle chick servers and find them very satisfactory.

Raw, lean meat is very fine food when it can be obtained without costing too much, although our work is very successful without it. It was not used this season in our home yard, where we raised so many chickens without loss and in perfect condition.

FEEDING THE FIRST THREE WEEKS.

The chicken that is properly handled the first week of its life is practically half raised. Like incubation, if the first week's work is properly done, the results are reasonably sure and the work easy; if not, the proper conditions may never be expected to exist with a lot of chickens that have been improperly handled the first week.

After the first week the bread and milk may be discontinued, although one feeding a day would be an advantage where the supply may be had at not too great an expense.

A part of the coop should have an earth bottom, and if the ground is hard and stony, it should be dug up and removed, and good garden soil and sand put in, to the depth of eight inches, and frequently spaded, so that the chicks can easily scratch for the grain you bury. It will aid digestion and strengthen the legs, which will be necessary to keep pace with the rapidly increasing weight of the body. Some of the chick food should be thoroughly mixed in the soil every day. It will keep them hustling to find the little seeds and finely cracked grain.

Never attempt to raise chickens in cellars, or any place below the surface of the ground.

FEEDING FROM THREE TO EIGHT WEEKS.

After they are three weeks old, all chickens that are intended for breeders or to stock the egg farm should be fed to produce bone and muscle rather than flesh. They take on fat readily during the next few weeks, and unless properly fed are likely to get too heavy for their legs, and also to be troubled with indigestion, either of which will retard the growth and make seconds of chickens that should stand in the front rank.

After they are three weeks old they should be fed as many kinds of small grain as you can get, including cracked corn for the night food. This should be given in the morning and at night. During the day they have all the dry wheat bran they will eat, and a very little chick food is raked in the run to keep them busy. Green food or finely cut clover is supplied every day. A very little meat scraps or fresh lean meat is excellent, but not altogether necessary, unless in case of weakness in the parent stock caused by insufficient or improper feeding. When the meat is not supplied, either sweet or granulated milk should be fed. Unless there is an abundant supply of natural grit, the manufactured kind should be fed liberally.

FROM EIGHT WEEKS TO MATURITY.

When the chicken has been properly handled until eight weeks old, its whole nature soon changes and the food given all goes to build up the frame. At this age they will stand very heavy feeding without injury, or adding to their flesh; in fact, it is very difficult to keep them in good condition for market or table, as the tendency is to grow lean and lank rather than fat.

In order to keep up the rapid pace of development it is necessary to tempt their appetite by feeding moistened mash for the morning food and also late at night so that there will be some for the early morning before the attendant has put in an appearance.

The mash should consist of equal parts by measure of ground oats, wheat bran and corn meal, and at least as much cut clover, alfalfa, or lawn clippings as all these others, and as much more as you can induce the chicks to eat. The whole should be moistened with milk and seasoned with a little salt. Water may be used instead of milk, but milk is better. We use sweet milk in winter and sour in summer. When the milk cannot be had, some granulated milk, fresh lean meat, or meat scraps should be fed in small quantities.

At noon they are given whole oats that have been covered with water since morning. After the first week the oats may be fed dry.

Dry wheat bran, green food or cut clover must be fed to furnish the bulk and keep them in perfect condition.

Cracked corn is fed late in the afternoon before giving the mash for night. In this way they are induced to eat more than they otherwise would, should the mash and cracked corn be fed at the same time.

The success of the work depends entirely upon the amount of food they can be made to consume and digest. Besides the quick development, we get hens better adapted for large egg yields, as all food not required to keep up the system must be turned into eggs, and the amount of the egg yield depends entirely upon the amount of food the hen can be made to consume.

FEEDING FOR EARLY MATURITY.

The pullets are now three months old, and have been fed in a manner to develop the frame with large strong bones, lacking only the filling out to make perfectly matured birds.

Our aim now is to feed all we can get them to eat of as many kinds of food as we can get, consisting of whole grain, ground food, shell, green food, etc. The time of the day for feeding the different kinds of food does not matter very much if they get whole grain at night with a liberal amount of corn. To determine when they are properly fed, the condition of the crop at roosting time and in the early morning will tell the story. When ready for the roosts the crops should be completely filled and rather hard, and in the morning they should be comparatively empty.

When the crops are not completely filled at night there is something lacking in the bill of fare that they need, and they should be tried with a little of everything we have to feed until they get what they are so much in need of. The bulky food should be given largely during the early part of the day, as it is easily digested, giving them a good appetite for the more substantial food later in the day.

When food is found in the crop in the early morning there should be more gravel or grit fed, and for this we prefer ground oyster or clam shells in addition to the gravel, as it supplies lime besides digestive material in larger quantities than obtained from the crushed stone, marble, or granite. When this fails to bring the desired results, less solid food should be given them, and more of the bulky food. Cases of indigestion are seldom found when they have access to the dry wheat bran.

The wet mash should be fed at least once each day, either in the morning or at noon, consisting of equal parts by measure of ground oats, wheat bran, corn meal, and as much clover or alfalfa as all these other things. Skim milk may be used to moisten this mixture, or water, if milk cannot be had.

The mash should be seasoned with a little salt and a very little pepper, either black or red, but not more than would be used to season food for the table.

Dry wheat bran and whole oats should be kept before them all of the time.

One of the most difficult tasks is grading the chickens without discarding valuable birds, and doing the work in time to fit the seconds for two-pound broilers when but eight weeks old.

The color of the eyes sometimes changes when they are from eight to ten weeks old, so it will be necessary to do some guess work in grading three-weeks-old chickens regarding the color of the eyes. The ear-lobes also change and take on the final color when from eight to ten weeks old.

The color of the feathers on buff and white breeds should be good when the chicken is small and the feathers just starting although there is often a slight change in color when they take on their adult plumage. The best specimens may be selected when they are but three weeks old. The legs and beak change some after this age, still they are beginning to take on the final color, and a very fair conclusion may be arrived at.

It is not difficult after a little practice to tell about what the comb will be, and all birds not strictly up to your expectations in that respect should be turned into broilers, excepting the early

Sunflowers Are Planted Along One Side of the Coops to Provide Shade

34

The Philo System

pullets that are bred for eggs, as they should be retained regardless of the required standard qualities.

The utility birds are more easily selected at a very young age as those looking the brightest and the ones maturing in advance of others of the same age will always make the hustling hens. They should have a bright keen eye, be quick in motion, and the first to reach the feed when it is given them. These will be the last to go to the roost at night, and the first to put in an appearance in the morning.

TWO POUND BROILERS IN EIGHT WEEKS.

The care of the chickens during the first three weeks is the same as before described, and the work of finishing up the broilers is accomplished in the following five weeks.

After the first three weeks they should be fed little and often, five times daily to get the best development in the shortest space of time.

All food should be moistened with milk excepting the cracked corn fed at night and the dry wheat bran that is constantly before them. Sweet milk to drink, as well as water, should be given to get the best quality and largest quantity at the proper age.

The mash at first should consist of equal parts, by measure of corn meal, ground oats and wheat bran, and as much clover or alfalfa as they can be induced to eat. When they are four weeks old gradually change the bran for middlings, until one-sixth of the mash is composed of middlings; when six weeks old gradually increase the amount of corn meal and add a little linseed meal to the mixture

All moistened food for chicks or fowls should be slightly salted as for table use.

The chicks should be provided with cut clover, or other green food in addition to what is in the mash.

When forcing for heavy weight they must be kept on the ground to prevent leg weakness. The ground should be spaded every day and not allowed to get wet from a soaking rain.

When the feeding has been properly handled the crops should be full at night. If they are not full, and the chicks are not inclined to fill them, a little less food should be given during the day, and gradually increased until the last feeding time at night.

When broilers are allowed to roam the fields they develop their leg muscles, which become tough and their flesh will be nearly as hard as that of older fowls. A broiler raised by our system is as tender as a squab, and the quality cannot be excelled.

In a few instances we have raised broilers weighing a little over two pounds in seven weeks.

A BROILER FARM ON A CITY LOT.

In answer to many inquiries regarding the possibilities of the broiler business on a city lot, we are herewith giving figures made from the results of tests made repeatedly, to show what may be accomplished on a city lot, fifty feet square. containing 2,500 square feet of ground.

These figures may appear exaggerated to many; still they are not overestimated, as we do not allow as much space here in actual practice. However, it is best to allow this space for the alleys on account of saving labor in the care of growing chickens. It is also possible to increase the number of finished broilers from twenty to twenty-five to the coop, adding twenty per cent. to gross receipts. In making the estimate, liberal allowance has been made for mortality, allowing twenty per cent. loss, while in actual practice here, and also in many other places where this system is being used, the mortality is less than five per cent.

The writer had the pleasure, recently, of showing Mr. J. W. Froley, of the U. S. Department of Agriculture, our small city plant and the broilers being raised by the new system. In one section of the chicken department we had a little over 200 pounds of broilers, and the total amount of ground occupied with the coops and walk is twenty feet long by five feet wide. These chickens, however, are past the broiler age, as they will now weigh a little over four pounds each, and the figures given are simply to show that former estimates as to the amount of poultry that can be successfully raised on a given space of ground are far from reaching the limit of possibilities.

All of the work necessary could be accomplished by one man, and we are not sure but one good, active woman would have still better success, as women are more likely to look after the little details, which are very essential during the first week of the chicken's life. With the help of a man one day in the week to do some heavy work and cleaning, it would not be very difficult to handle the plant, although very confining, possibly more so than the average person would care to undertake.

It would also be possible for a very strong, active man to care for this plant so as to produce the eggs necessary to use from which to hatch the chickens, and one is more likely to succeed when getting eggs from his own hens than where it is necessary

Ground plan of a city lot, showing the arrangement of sixty Philo System coops and walks, where $1,450.00 worth of broilers can be raised in eight months on a city lot fifty feet square.

to purchase the eggs. However, it is possible to arrange with some good, reliable farmer to raise the eggs, even though it may be necessary to furnish him with the kind of breeding stock desired for broilers. We sometimes furnish the breeders and pay the farmer a little above the market price for the eggs produced by our hens, with the understanding that they are to be fed exactly as we feed to produce eggs capable of hatching chickens which will develop into finished broilers in the shortest space of time.

Our average hatches have been better than 85 per cent. during the past several years; still in making the figures we only estimate on 50 per cent. hatches, making it necessary to set 50 eggs per day to hatch 25 chickens to keep all coops filled. After the first chickens hatched are two months old, twenty or more two-pound broilers would be ready for market daily. This would allow for twenty per cent. mortality, which is greatly in excess of our losses, and also make a daily output of forty pounds of finished broilers including Sundays; although the Sunday chickens should be sold on the following Monday, making the amount 80 pounds in place of 40 pounds as on all other days.

Commencing to hatch chickens by January 1st, the first large broilers would be ready to market about the first of March. In many markets there is a demand for broilers about half the weight of the two-months broilers, and many could be sold by February 15th, bringing as much per chicken as they would when fully two months old. While this would add to the income of the plant, we will omit it from the estimate as the returns made from the regular line will be in excess of former estimates, and will be doubted by many who do not know the possibilities. A visit to our small city plant here has convinced the most skeptical that we can do all we are claiming, and are now doing a little more.

During March and April 20 broilers per day can be marketed at 50 cents each. In May and June they should bring 40 cents each, and in July and August about 30 cents, making a total income during the six months of $1,450.00. At the very high price of all kinds of grain and the necessary food the cost of feeding, and eggs for incubation, should not exceed $576.00, leaving a balance of $874.00 net profit. This is not all, as 600 capons could be matured in the same plant, using the cockerels in the last lot of broilers for capons, which should be developed to weigh from eight to twelve pounds by January 1st, or by the time of starting the broilers for another year. This should add at least $300.00 to the profits of the plant.

In our plant here we matured ten of the late hatched pullets in each of the brooder coops, and many of them were laying in coops during the coldest winter weather.

Several tons of the best fertilizer would be made which should also add much to the income of the plant.

Now about the investment. We will take it for granted that the party operating the plant owns a plot of ground fifty feet square, or that this small space is included when renting a house in which to live. However, extra rent could be paid and there would still be left more clear money than 99 per cent. of the laboring people make.

The material for the brooder coops and small boxes for brooders could be bought for about $350.00, and 21 cycle Hatchers at wholesale prices for $84.00. In addition to these amounts $80.00 would be required for food until the first sales were made, making a total investment of $514.00. This is a comparatively small amount of capital to invest in a plant that promises so well in returns.

With the former ways of handling the business there is a constant danger of loss by fire and of injuring the chickens by lamps, which sometimes get unreliable. By the improved method all the danger from fire is eliminated, besides the loss caused so many times from hawks, cats, dogs and other prowling animals.

Just a word of caution in conclusion, as we do not wish anyone to think such returns would be possible without some experience or knowledge of the work. Although there is not the first thing that any ordinarily bright person could not do after a little experience, it would be very unwise to attempt the work in a large way without first mastering the little details by putting into actual test the smallest unit of this plant. If, by its use, you can accomplish very nearly as good results as we are getting here, producing forty pounds of broilers in each single coop in eight weeks, you will not have any difficulty in developing the plant to the full capacity and do even better than we are now doing.

HOW TO GET LARGE EGG YIELDS.

In the directions for the care of breeding stock the essential points for getting large egg yields are well covered. Larger yields may be had by increasing the amount of meat scraps and providing sweet milk after the cream has been removed. The milk will not injure the quality of the eggs for incubation, neither will fresh, lean meat. Commercial meat scraps when not composed entirely of lean meat will injure the quality of eggs for hatching when fed in quantities to get the largest egg yield.

The best egg yields are obtained where the hens have an abundance of bulky food, clean water, oyster shells, sweet milk fresh lean meat, a large variety of grain, dry wheat bran, and a comfortable roosting place. Never feed laying hens by measure. Give them all they will eat or you cannot get the best egg yield. See that the hens are provided with all the above, and your egg basket will be well filled.

HOW TO GET EGGS WHEN PRICES ARE HIGH.

Change the Season for Hatching and the Hens Will Molt in the Spring as Naturally as They Now Molt in the Fall.

Poultry keepers who are satisfied to handle poultry just as their grandfathers handled it must be content when selling eggs at the lowest market price. However, this is not necessary, as recent discoveries are changing conditions which cause the hens to be more productive in the early winter and molt during the spring months.

We all know that hens as commonly bred are more productive in the spring and early summer than at any other time of year. This is the natural breeding season, and they lay during these months just because their mothers did, making it difficult to convince them that the time they should do their best is during the fall and winter months.

It would probably be safe to estimate that 99 per cent of the hens raised for laying are hatched during May and June, and our plan is to hatch them at the season of the year we wish them to be most productive.

It requires some little effort and quite a bit of skill to bring about the changes necessary to cause the breeding fowls to produce fertile, hatchable eggs at this unnatural time, and the first efforts in this direction are the least successful. Each succeeding year shows a decided improvement caused by using only the early-hatched cockerels and pullets for the breeders, and being particular to carry at least two lines of fowls not nearly related, that out-crosses may be had each season without the necessity of purchasing breeders which have not been hatched during the early winter. The third season will show a marked degree of improvement, and hatchable eggs will be more easily obtained.

Should every farmer and poultryman adopt the plan, the time for high-priced eggs would soon be changed to the spring months, as every one would have eggs to sell during the winter. This, however, will never happen, as there are but few people who would ever believe in the possibility of making such radical changes, as compared with the multitude of poultry keepers who would doubt the advisability of being progressive along any line that would change the natural instinct and habits of hens.

All this talk is not theory. It is the result of patience and perseverance in endeavoring to change the breeding season from March, April and May to December, January and February.

Several years ago we commenced setting eggs January 20th, hatching chickens February 10th. At first it was very difficult to get hatchable eggs at this season of the year. A few of the February hatched chickens were selected for the next winter's breeders, and the eggs were 75 per cent. fertile and hatched well, and the chickens showed more strength than those of the previous year, while the eggs from later-hatched breeders were hardly worth setting, although from the same strain of fowls, and fed and cared for just as those producing the better eggs. This commenced to open our eyes, and we were still more surprised the following year to find nearly every egg capable of producing a strong, healthy chicken.

Our first winter-hatched chickens last season were forced for early egg production, and were laying at a lively rate during July and August and in fact all the fall, when eggs were selling at forty to fifty cents per dozen, and we never had hens more productive during the months of April and May. December 10th thirty-nine eggs were started to incubate to test the fertility, and from these, twenty-seven sturdy chickens hatched January 1st. They were placed out of doors January 2nd without artificial heat and were raised almost without loss. At this writing, May 1st, the average weight is four pounds. The cockerels weighing four and one-half pounds and the three pullets three and one-half pounds each.

From this experience we have learned several things: First, that by proper selection and breeding, eggs may be produced that will hatch as well in January, and the chickens will be as strong, as those hatched in June; second, that chickens may be raised with the least trouble without artificial heat during the coldest winter weather; third, that the surplus brings the highest market price, and that the pullets will do most of the laying during the time eggs are worth gathering. And this is not all. When the pullets are kept in condition to lay all through the winter they will molt during the spring and will then be in condition to lay valuable eggs during the fall and winter while the spring-hatched hens are resting.

Our pullets that were laying last July are now in the full molt, which is conclusive evidence that we are not laboring under a mistake, and also that changing the season for hatching will also change the season of greatest productiveness.

Like many other valuable discoveries, this has all come about while working for other purposes, especially to get show birds that would be fully developed for the August and September shows, and not trying to breed them to lay during the unnatural season. Still the results from the out-of-season work have been more valuable to us along unexpected lines than the purpose for which we were striving.

SUMMER AND FALL CHICKENS.

All chickens hatched by July 1st can be fully matured before the extreme cold of winter sets in, and will make valuable poultry for late breeders or for laying market eggs.

In this section of the country it is difficult to raise chickens during July and August when given free range, as the insects are too numerous and many of them are very injurious, causing bowel trouble, which results in the loss of many chicks. When confined to the coops we recommend, and the coops are protected from the direct rays of the sun, the chickens will mature as rapidly and make as good poultry as those hatched during the earlier months. Berry bushes, lima beans or sun flowers make good shade, and when the rows are planted six feet apart the coops may be moved between the rows. Beans and sun flowers may be planted in the same hill or drill, and you will not have to set poles, as the sunflowers grow tall and answer the purpose very nicely.

It will be better for the farmers who wish to allow the chicks free range to set as many eggs as possible from the first to the tenth of August. The chicks will then hatch just before the first of September and, with proper care, will grow and develop more rapidly than at any other season of the year. The cockerels will be just in time for the Thanksgiving market and the pullets can be wintered cheaply and will commence laying in the early spring, making the very best summer layers, in fact, continuing to lay after the earlier hatched have stopped.

PEDIGREE BREEDING.

It is safe to estimate that not over one poultry keeper in a thousand can tell the father and mother of each chicken raised or who can tell just what to expect from the results of mating more than two or three hens in a flock. If we are to reach the success we are striving for it is very important that we know the exact breeding of every chicken raised so as to be able to take advantage of our season's work and know about what to expect from a certain line of mating.

At the beginning of the season we were determined to be systematic and that we would know at the end of the season the father and mother of each chicken raised. We used all the sixteen toe marks, but soon learned that it would be necessary to mark the chickens in other ways if we were to keep an accurate record of all the chickens.

During the present year we have already mated each of our five best exhibition hens to four of our best exhibition males. With these several matings it has been necessary to have four distinct marks for each of the five hens, making twenty in all, to keep an accurate record showing the ancestors of each chicken raised. After all the sixteen toe marks had been used we commenced using aluminum pigeon bands, which are simply pressed together and may be expanded as the legs of the chickens develop. When the chickens are banded, the records are made by using the number on the band to distinguish the chickens.

To be accurate and know the sire of every chicken, it is necessary to incubate the eggs as long as the fertility lasts before starting the next mating, when fertile eggs may be expected in three days.

When several hundred chickens are banded it is quite a task to see that the bands are not too tight. At the time of expanding the bands (which is necessary about once every two weeks) we get much pleasure in consulting the records and noting the development and markings of the chickens from certain matings, and we soon learn the source from which the best chickens come, giving us an opportunity to produce more chickens from the same line before the close of the season, and to discard all breeders failing to produce strong, healthy chickens of the quality desired and those not maturing properly.

When the chickens have outgrown the pigeon bands, larger ones must be substituted, and the new numbers recorded in their proper place.

When attempting this work with twelve to fifteen males and nearly a hundred females to select from, much thought and study are necessary to get the best results and to get the majority of the chickens from the breeders producing the best specimens.

The only advantage we have been able to find in breeding old fowls is in knowing just what to expect from certain matings. This may be good practice to a certain extent; still by so doing we are satisfied to leave "well enough" alone and are not taking advantage of the opportunity to raise better poultry. If we are doing the work properly there should be an improvement in each generation, and to use last season's breeders we are just one year behind.

LEG WEAKNESS.

Winter chicks are often troubled with a weakness of the legs, and some times the toes will turn under until they lose the use of their feet. Indigestion is the cause, and the best remedy is to stop all fattening food such as corn and corn meal. Give plenty of ground oats, wheat bran and milk, until they have recovered the use of their feet, then feed but sparingly of rich foods and those hard to digest.

Leg weakness is seldom, if ever, found when the chicks are on the ground, and when it is possible to keep them there it is much better than on board floors.

GAPES.

When ground once becomes infected with gape worms, it is very difficult to keep chicks free from the pests. The freezing of the ground during the winter does not kill the worms, and the chicks that have access to the infected ground soon become afflicted. If only a few are troubled, most of them may be saved by removing the worms from the windpipes of the chicks with a horse-hair or fine wire. But if they are put into our anti-lice brooder, they may be more quickly treated. Sprinkle air-slaked lime and pulverized sulphur on the cloth cover of the brooder. When the chicks move about in the brooder the lime is sifted through the cloth, causing the chicks to inhale a little of it during the night. A very little of the lime should be used at a time, so as not to smother the chicks. The same treatment is also good for colds, canker, etc.

When fresh ground from the field is supplied for the brooder runs to a depth of about ten inches, your chicks will never have the gapes.

LICE.

Sprinkle a little lice powder on the brooder cloth over the chickens and there will be no lice.

When the buildings are overrun with lice the best remedy is boiling water. Thoroughly drench the inside of the building with dipperfuls of boiling water. Do not use a spray, as the water will cool before reaching the lice.

Dissolve as much salt as possible in the water and one treatment will generally last a full season.

Old fowls dusting in wood ashes will be free from lice

Birds-eye View of the Original Philo System Plant

46

BROODING CHICKENS WITHOUT ARTIFICIAL HEAT.

Thousands of chickens are raised every year without artificial heat. It is not a new discovery, as it has been practiced in China and Egypt many centuries, yet Americans, usually quick to take advantage of improved methods, have been slow in discovering the advantages of this system. We as Americans are not satisfied to accomplish things in a small way like our ancient friends, and have endeavored to devise appliances whereby the chickens may be turned out like the output of great factories. Although the output may be unlimited, nature has something to say when its laws are violated to any great extent. Raising the chickens is not at all unlike hatching them. By furnishing a little higher degree of heat than is given the eggs under natural conditions we hasten the process of incubation from twenty-four to forty-eight hours and get bright, healthy looking youngsters until the time arrives for them to derive nourishment from the absorbed yolk, when excessive heating having hardened the yolk, the chick must soon perish. Chickens thrive for a time when subjected to a temperature above that supplied by the mother hen, still the bad effects are soon discovered and the chicken dwindles without any apparent cause. Nature also rebels when the number of chickens in one flock is greatly in excess of those raised under natural conditions.

We have raised chickens successfully for many years without supplying heat, and in many instances where the temperature would drop below zero for a week at a time, and without loss or bad effect on any of the chickens. Until the last few years our experiments have been too elaborate and complicated to be practical. All that is really required is a very simple device by which the natural heat of the chicken is retained.

The plan we give in this book is very simple, yet the proper conditions may be had for successful work, and without the danger so common and fatal with the average artificially heated brooder.

We are not surprised that people generally are slow to believe it possible to brood baby chickens successfully during the coldest winter weather out of doors without artificial heat, and were it not for the fact that they are thus grown right under our own eyes we might be as slow as others to think it possible to accomplish the work in a satisfactory manner.

While writing this for the book in a comfortable office by the side of a warm fire—there are about forty baby chickens in one flock now only two days old just a few feet away out of doors in the brooders without artificial heat. There are also several other flocks one week old, two weeks old, three weeks old, etc , until reaching maturity. Since the two younger lots have been hatched and placed in the yard the weather has been cloudy and very cold with only one day of partial sunshine. Several mornings have found the temperature at zero, and yesterday it was 12° below. A heavy fall of snow last night and today has nearly covered the brooder coops, the glass is thickly covered with frost, yet the chickens in the frosted coops, now only a few days old, are as bright and lively as crickets.

It has required many years of study and experimenting to give the writer courage to make the trial during the extreme winter weather, although it has been a success during the spring and summer for many years past.

Hardly a day passes when people are not here from hundreds of miles away to see the tiny living balls of downy chickens in their snow-bound quarters, as chipper and bright as snow birds on a cold winter's day.

All conditions must be absolutely correct to be successful during the coldest weather. To get these results the details of the work as set forth in this article must be carefully followed or there will be a lot of frozen chickens and disappointed poultry keepers. One party who was very anxious to try brooding without heat, during one of the coldest days last winter placed two chickens, just hatched, out of doors, without heat early in the morning before going to work. On returning at noon the chickens were found right where they had been left and were frozen until they were as hard as the heart of the thoughtless keeper. Had he profited by what he had read he would have known that it required at least twenty-five chickens to furnish the necessary heat to keep them warm.

In the first place we will take up the construction of the latest brooder coops just as they are now being used by us with the best success, and hope to mak it so plain that additional information will not be necessary.

BROODER COOP CONSTRUCTION:—Hemlock lumber is used for the foundation, as it will last longer when placed on the ground than any other kind of inexpensive lumber. The box part of the brooder coops is made of North Carolina pine, as good, sound boards twelve inches wide can be bought at a lower price than any other kind of lumber, and when it is painted inside and outside it will last many years. The strips for the tops and sliding frames are made of soft pine or native poplar, either of which will hold a nail without splitting and are light to handle and durable. We use one-ply Paroid roofing for floors and two-ply for the roof.

New Style Philo System Brooder Coop

50

The Philo System

The center partition is held in position with cleats so it can be easily removed when not required to retain the heat for the little chickens.

FOUNDATION:—The foundation frames are made of 1x4 in. lumber just the size of the coop, six feet long and three feet wide outside with a four inch partition in the center. In one end of the coop the floor is laid on strips about one and one-half inches from the bottom to keep the boards off the ground and prevent them from getting damp. The floor is then covered with one-ply roofing material that the moisture from the top may not penetrate the boards when the litter becomes damp.

The coops and foundations were formerly made of square edged boards. We are now making them ship lapped to hold the sections and foundations together without being nailed, and to prevent the storms and wind from going through the open cracks which are likely to appear when square-edged boards are used. Any lumber dealer will understand the term ship lap, so that you will not have any trouble in getting this kind of lumber.

COOPS:—The brooder coop is the exact size of the foundation frame, three feet wide and six feet long. The boards are ship lapped on the bottom edge to fit over the foundation. The back board is twelve inches wide and the two ends and center boards are one and one-quarter inches narrower to allow room for the sliding frame and three-eighths of an inch between the frame and the cover for ventilation when the coop is closed on very cold nights. An opening four inches square is cut in the partition board for the chickens to pass from one end of the coop to the other. A sash one foot wide by six feet long, having six panes of glass, is used to form the front of the coop, and the bottom of of the sash is also rabbetted to fit the foundation. Parting strips 1-2x7-8 in., which are used in building window frames, may be had at almost any lumber yard. These are nailed lengthwise on the inside of the back board and the inside top edge of the sash 1 1-4 in. down from the top so that they will come level with the ends of the coop for the muslin frame to slide on.

SLIDING FRAME:—The muslin frame is made of 7-8 x1 1-2in. strips of lumber mitered at the corner and with a center piece of the same material to strengthen the long sides. The frame is covered with one-inch wire netting and over this is tacked an inexpensive grade of unbleached muslin. The entire frame is covered for cold weather or where the climate is cold, but during warm weather only one-half of the frame is covered with muslin. This frame may be made of 1-2x1 1-2 or 2 in. strips and lapped at the corners instead of mitering, which might be easier for some people who are not accustomed to this kind of work.

We are now putting the Paroid on top of the frame work instead of on the under side with three strips on top as described below.

In making the roof two strips 6 ft. 2 in. long are used, the front one 3 in. wide, and the back one 2 in. For the ribs on the under side we use eight strips 2 ft. 9 in. long and 2 in. wide, and one strip 2 ft. 9 in. long and 3 in. wide. For the top we use two strips 3 ft. 2 in. long and 2 in. wide, and one strip 3 ft. 2 in. long and 3 in. wide. All these are 7-8 in. thick.

The Paroid is 3 ft. wide and we cut two pieces 3 ft. 2 in. long. The ends of each piece of Paroid are nailed to the long strips, with the outer edge of each piece even with the ends of the long strips. This makes the roof 6 ft. 2 in. long and 3 ft. 2 in. wide, with a two in. open space in the center between the two pieces of Paroid.

Now turn the roof over and nail the nine 2 ft. 9 in. strips (the 3 in. one in the center) between the inside edges of the long strips. These shorter strips should be cut so as to crowd the long strips apart and stretch the Paroid to remove all wrinkles. When these strips are all nailed in their places, turn the roof over again and nail the Paroid to these short strips, taking pains to see that the inside edges are securely fastened to the 3 in. strip. Fill the space between these edges with roofing cement or paint, and also let it come over a little on each edge. You now have left the three 3 ft. 2 in. strips; nail the 3 in. strip over this center space, and a 2 in. strip at each end. This will now be the top of the roof, with three strips showing over the Paroid, while the under-side will have two long strips and nine short ones. This arrangement makes the roof absolutely water-proof.

A strip of wood 1-2 in. thick by 1 1-2 in. wide and 3 feet long is used to hold the roof in any desired position. A small hole is bored through one end of the stick to fasten it to the top edge of front sash. The hole should be large enough to allow the stick to move at any angle without binding, but not so much that it will slide off the head of the screw. Several larger holes are bored in the stick so that they will slide over the head of the screw in the center of the front edge of the roof, that it may be adjusted at any desired angle, as it is sometimes advisable to change the adjustment in varied weather conditions. When the sun shines the roof should be wide open and when it is stormy, it should be nearly closed, but not entirely closed unless the weather is very cold.

HOW TO SET THE COOPS:—The ground should be nearly level where the coop is set. If the ground is frozen hard it will not matter, as the sun shining through the sash will soon draw the frost, and the little chicks over the board floor will not suffer even though the ground is frozen solid.

The coop should be placed so it will face the south during the winter, and if possible where there will not be any obstruction to prevent what little sunshine there is from entering the coop.

The roof should be opened when the sun is shining, to dry out the cloth and give all the ventilation it is possible to give them without exposure. When the sun is not shining, and at night, the roof should be closed, unless the night is warm, when it may be left open about six inches. During the warm weather the coop should face the north, and the roof will shield the chickens from the direct rays of the sun.

When there is twice as much ground as required for coops it might be an advantage to move the coops once each week to give the ground a chance to purify itself by absorbing the ammonia and decomposed matter from the droppings, requiring less spading to keep everything in a perfectly sanitary condition.

It is not uncommon to find filthy conditions in poultry yards where valuable stock is being raised, when a few minutes properly used every day would keep everything in fine order.

The cover is used as a protection against storm and against the direct rays of the sun, when too warm for the comfort of the chickens, and may be lifted to any desired angle to make the chickens comfortable with unfavorable weather conditions. When the chicks are very young the cover is let down flat at night to retain the heat.

The cost of this brooder coop is not over half the cost of coops commonly used for the same purpose. The chickens are at all times in the best possible condition to raise them practically without loss.

For an experiment a cockerel weighing about three pounds was taken from one of the coops and given his liberty and the free run of the garden. In just a month he gained one pound in weight, while those confined in the coops gained one and a half pounds each. This bird was given the same kind of food as those confined, besides having the pick of the garden.

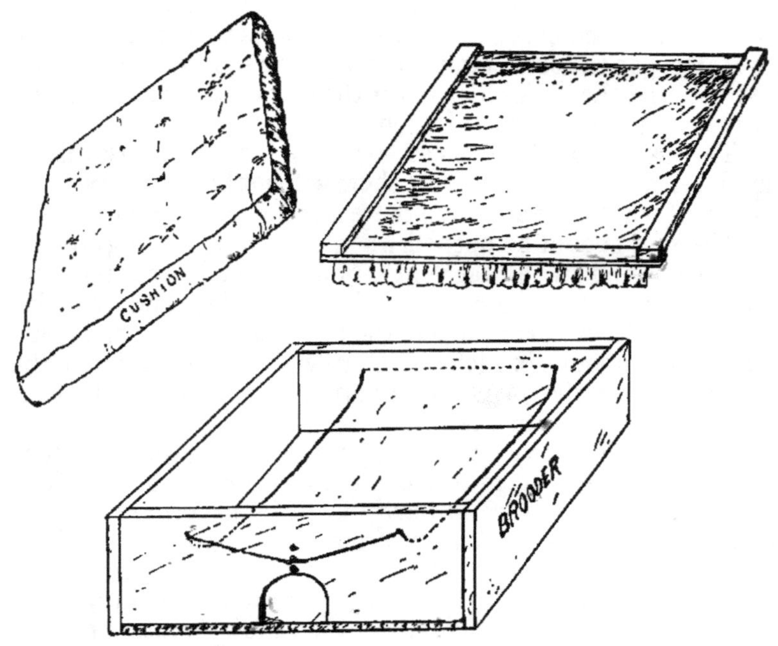

BROODER WITHOUT ARTIFICIAL HEAT.

BROODER BOX CONSTRUCTION:—Make a box of half-inch or thicker lumber eighteen inches square inside and eight inches deep. Cover the bottom of the box with water-proof roofing material so that it may be easily cleaned and to prevent the bottom board from getting damp. Cut an opening in the center of one side of the box three and one-half inches square for the chickens to enter.

Make a frame of one-half inch by one inch strips of lumber a little less than eighteen inches square so it will fit loosely in the brooder box. The corners of the frame may be lapped and nailed, or mitered. Tack a piece of unbleached muslin or cotton cloth on the underside of the frame so it will sag in the center about two inches below the frame. This is best accomplished by making half-inch plaits in the cloth about two inches from each corner of the frame. Small nails may be partially driven on the inside of the box to hold the frame at the desired height.

A View of the Poultry Yard of the Philo National Poultry Institute, Elmira, N. Y.

The Philo System

Three cushions are made of muslin or cotton cloth eighteen inches square, or just the right size to fill the box, and each of these is filled with about one-half pound of cotton, so when finished they will be about one inch thick. The three cushions should weigh about one and one-half pounds. They should be tied as in making comfortables to hold the cotton in place. The cushions are the only tops to the brooder boxes and are better than to have a board cover.

This brooder box will accomodate about fifty chickens at first and from twenty-five to thirty when they are four weeks old. It will brood twenty-five chickens as long as they require brooding during the coldest weather. The brooder is to be used inside the brooder coop, which will afford ample protection for the chicks.

THE BEST WAY TO LEARN HOW:—While it is possible to raise the finest chickens during the coldest weather without artificial heat, it is somewhat safer and easier to keep them in the "Metal Mother" at first (which is supplied with heat and automatically regulated) until they are about one week old. They learn to go into the heated brooders with less teaching, and when about one week old the lampless brooders will be more readily accepted.

After having a little experience in brooding without heat there will not be any difficultyin placing the chickens in the lampless brooders as soon as hatched, even during the coldest weather.

There should never be less than 25 chickens at first when the weather is freezing cold, and when it is zero weather there should be about 40, and when it is 25 below zero there should be 50 chickens in each brooder. Although it might be possible to brood them out of doors without heat when it is colder than 25 degrees below zero, we haven't made the test, as this is about the coldest weather we ever have in this locality.

In testing the work where it is much colder, we would carry the chickens into the house at night, brooder box and all, and only place them out in the brooder coop when the sun is shining, untilthey are old enough to stand the cold and keep comfortably warm at night when in the brooder box.

When there are but few chickens to brood and the weather is very cold they should only be placed out of doors when the sun is shining,until they are about one week old, or large enough to keep warm without being carried into the house.

When the chicks are first hatched the box is filled to the cloth-covered frame with cut clover or other fine litter. A small nest is made in the center just large enough to hold the chickens, and as soon as the chickens are old enough to run out. a little depression is made in the litter to the opening of the brooder.

The litter should be changed as often as it becomes damp which is about once the first week and twice each week when the chickens are older.

Place the cloth-covered frame in the brooder box so the lower part of the cloth will just touch the litter, which should be at least once inch deep in the center of the box and much deeper around the sides of the box. Over this place one cushion at first when the weather is warm, two cushions when it is freezing, and three cushions for zero weather. The correct number ot cushions to use after the chickens are older can only be determined by the number of chickens in the brooder, their size and the condition of the weather. The desired conditions can best be learned by running the hand through the small opening in the box after the chickens have been in it for about one hour. When they are found crowded together and there is evidence of moisture, the cushions should be lowered to keep out circulating air, thereby inducing the chickens to spread out rather than to huddle. The top cushion will become quite damp and should be placed out in the sun and air to dry two or three times weekly. A few extra cushions will be found very handy.

During zero weather when the chickens are first hatched the small opening in the side of the box should be banked with clover to keep out the cold air. If the clover is dry there will not be any danger of smothering the chickens, as the ventilation through it will give them all the air they require on a zero night, and the opening should never be closed in any other way. The brooder should always be used in the brooder coop, made after the plans as set forth in this book.

The brooder box should be placed in the end of the brooder coop, having a floor and dry litter, and the chickens confined to this end of the coop, until they are old enough to find their way back to the brooder, which is generally in about three days after being hatched. The cut clover or litter should be about one inch thick over the floor of the coop, and should be changed as often as it becomes damp.

The chickens are always fed in the brooder coop outside of the brooder box, even during the coldest weather, which will not injure them in the least, provided they find their way back soon after they have satisfied their hunger. The half of the brooder coop without the floor should be filled with finely sifted sand about four inches deep, so it will come about level with the floor and high enough above the ground to keep it reasonably dry. It is better, however, not to become perfectly dry, but should be just dry enough to keep it fine, and moist enough to sprout grain that should be mixed in with the sand each day. At first a very little chick food is sprinkled over the sand and slightly mixed with it so it will not be difficult for the chickens to find it. When kept busily at work scratching for the food, and provided with an abundance of dry wheat bran and sprouted oats they will never have indigestion, weak legs, or the blind staggers, which are common with winter chickens raised on board floors. (See page 29, Feeding The First Three Weeks.)

SUMMER COLONY COOP.

Every poultryman, farmer or fancier will find our light Summer Colony Coops of much value, even though our entire system is not adopted. They are especially well adapted for use as a desirable place to keep a small breeding pen from early Spring until the end of the season. They may also be used to the best advantage as a brooder coop, as well as for broody hens, fattening cockerels, maturing pullets, and growing capons.

The cost of material and labor to build this style of coop is not over half that required to build the Winter Colony Coop, and its value in a poultry plant can hardly be overestimated.

Two panels four feet wide and twelve feet long are used in forming the coop. Two three-cornered ends made with doors, and one partition covered with muslin, make the complete coop without furniture, the center partition being used only in cold weather to retain the heat while the fowls are roosting, or when used as a brooder coop to retain the heat for the chickens.

The lumber used is half or three-quarter inch strips two inches wide and four feet long running up and down; the ends are nailed to three by one inch strips twelve feet long. Heavy water-proof roofing material is used to enclose the ends, and six feet of the center is covered with one-inch mesh wire netting, making a roosting room, feed room and park. The one-inch mesh wire is used to keep sparrows out.

CONSTRUCTION OF SUMMER COLONY COOP.

To make the panels, mark out a place on the floor four feet wide by twelve feet long, and draw a four-feet cross line three feet from either end, leaving six feet in the center. By measuring with a rod about thirteen feet long from corner to corner in the form of a letter X you will get the panels perfectly square when the measurements are alike from either corner. Nail four or five cleats along each of the twelve feet lines, place the two-inch strip twelve feet long on one of the lines and the three-inch strip on the other. Cut roofing material that is three feet wide in strips four feet long, and one-inch mesh wire netting that is four feet wide in strips six feet three inches long. Tack the roofing and netting in place on one of the twelve-feet strips, then nail over this the six four-feet strips as indicated in the drawing. Nail the other end of the four-feet strips, and also the roofing and wire to the other long strip, drawing it tight and smooth. Turn the panel over and nail the roofing and netting to the four-feet strips, and the panel will be completed.

When two long panels have been completed, stand them up and fasten the top edges together, then spread the bottoms three feet six inches. You will then have the exact size and shape for the end panels. Make a drawing on the floor of this size. Lay a piece of ten-inch board along the bottom line, then hold over the long lines a straight-edge strip which will give the bevel to mark the ten-inch board, making a pattern to be used in marking out as many of the ten-inch boards as will be needed to complete the coops.

In the same manner lay a one by two-inch strip along the four-feet line, find the center of the bottom line which will be twenty-two inches from the corner, lay a strip over this line with the other end over a point where the two four-feet lines intersect; marking along this strip will give the correct miter for the upper corner, and a pattern to use in laying out the others. The doors are made in the same manner of a proper size to fit inside the other frame, and long enough to lap a half inch over the face side of the ten-inch base board.

The doors are covered with muslin or roofing material and hinged to the frame making the end panel.

When used early in the spring and late in the fall, panels four by six feet covered with roofing material are used over the netting to protect the birds from the rain and snow. They are fastened at the top with screw hooks or light hinges, and are raised at any desired angle to overcome unfavorable weather conditions.

The arrangement of the roosts, nests, etc., is plainly shown in the drawings.

HOW TO USE THE SUMMER COLONY COOP.

It is best to place this coop over mellow soil without grass sod, as the fowls require exercise to keep them in perfect condition. A handful of whole oats raked or spaded into the mellow

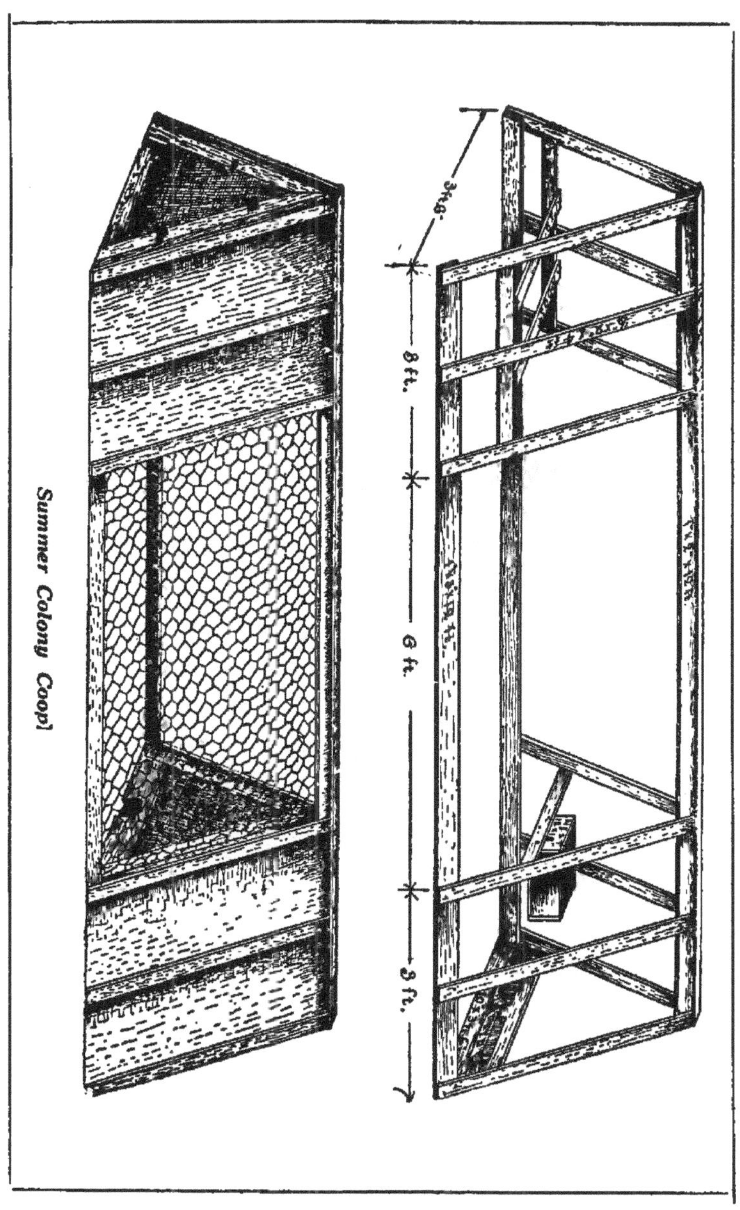

Summer Colony Coop]

soil every day will provide the necessary attraction and also some green food, as some of the grain will not be discovered until it sends forth a delicate sprout that is greatly relished.

When not limited for room, the most desirable conditions may be had by seeding to clover a strip of ground six feet wide by twenty-five feet long. One by six hemlock boards should be placed in the ground along either edge of the clover sod, extending about one inch above the sod to protect the edges from being scratched out. The colony coop is placed crosswise over the sod (when thoroughly established,) in a manner to bring the portion enclosed in the netting over the sod with the three feet on either end over the mellow soil for exercise and dusting. The coop is moved three and one-half feet, or just its width every day to give its occupants a fresh supply of clover, and also to prevent them from digging up the roots. The space of twenty-five feet will allow seven days for moving the coop without being in the same position any two days, allowing seven days to replenish the clover that is consumed in one day. This brings about ideal conditions for a breeding pen of six hens, and when they fail under such conditions to produce six eggs per day many days in the season, they have not been properly bred.

When limited for room the coop may be kept in one position during the entire season by thoroughly working the soil.

WINTER COLONY COOP.

In our Winter Colony Coop we have combined a complete poultry plant, especially well adapted for housing and yarding poultry of all ages from the day they are first hatched, at all seasons of the year, and in all weather conditions from the hottest summer days of the South to the coldest days of the extreme North. With this coop it is possible for parties renting property, and the city fancier limited for space, to raise as fine poultry, and get as good returns as the farmer who has unlimited range. The entire poultry plant is moved as easily as household furniture, and a day's notice (without handling a hen) will enable one to locate his plant many miles from the original site.

Many people refrain from keeping poultry on account of the cost of building, without any assurance of being able to dispose of the buildings at the original cost. With our system there will be a demand for the coops, when properly constructed of good materials, at nearly the original cost. The actual expense of building them to accommodate any number of hens is not over three-fourths as much as a large house would cost to accommodate the same number of fowls. The egg yield will be at least twenty-five per cent. greater than where twenty-five or fifty hens are kept in one flock, and a larger number of the chickens hatched may be raised, making better fowls than would be possible to raise under ordinary conditions.

The standard size of the coop is three feet wide, six feet long and three feet eight inches high to the eaves with a gable one foot higher, making the extreme height four feet eight inches to the top of the gable. It is made two stories high with nest boxes, roosts, feeding troughs, etc., on the second floor. Aside from the space required for nest boxes, stairs, etc., there is left about thirty square feet of floor space, which is ample room for six laying hens and one male bird, fifty chicks the first three weeks, or twenty-five chickens until they weigh three pounds each. Ffteen pullets may be matured until they are ready to lay, or twelve capons grown to perfection. These coops have many advantages, and were it not for the fact that they are more expensive to build, we should use more of them.

CONSTRUCTION.

They are made from half-inch, three-fourths or one-inch lumber either matched or square edged and dressed. When a good grade of matched lumber is used in the construction, and nicely painted they make a very attractive coop that does not look out of place in the best kept yards. When the cheaper grades of lumber are used it is necessary to cover the entire outside with water-proof roofing material, and when a good grade is used and nicely applied they are attractive and durable.

The ends are made three feet wide, three feet eight inches high to the eaves, and one foot higher to the top of the gable. One end is made solid with three cross cleats of one by two inch lumber, one being nailed at the bottom, one two feet from the bottom for the second floor to rest on and the other across to the eaves. The other end is made like a frame with three inch sides, three inch bottom and a gable, leaving an opening two feet six inches wide by three feet five high to be covered on the inside with muslin and wire netting to keep out dogs, cats, rats, etc. Extremely cold nights the coop is closed with the exception of this window which provides the necessary ventilation. Where the climate is very cold it is well to make a frame just the right size to fit this opening, covering it with muslin on the outside to keep out the cold. When in place there will be about an inch space between the two thicknesses of muslin covering the window opening.

Winter Colony Coop

The Philo System

The sides are composed of two panels twenty-two inches wide by six feet long and hinged in the center, the top half being secured with screws to the ends, and the bottom half left unfastened so it may be opened by swinging up from the bottom. Both sides are made alike, or if more light is desired in the lower story, the upper part of one of these sides may be made of a long sash, such as used in the brooder coop.

The floor for the second story is made three feet wide and five feet ten inches long, leaving an opening ten inches wide by twenty inches long at the window end for the stairs which are made from a board just wide enough to close the opening and three feet long. Cleats are nailed on to aid the chickens in climbing, and the board is hinged at the back end so it may be lifted on very cold nights to retain the heat, and closed while very young chickens are being raised in the upper story until they are large enough to use the stairs.

The back portion of the roof is covered with one panel two feet wide by six feet four inches long, allowing a projection of two inches at the eaves and over the gable ends. The front is the same length and two inches wider, and divided into two sections, that one may be raised at a time. They are cleated on the ends of the boards, as battens would interfere with the frames under them. They are hinged to the top of the back roof and allowed to extend over it one inch so there will be a one-inch lap when the front is open,to prevent the rain from leaking through.

Two frames are made of 7-8x1 1-2 inch lumber, mitered and nailed at the corners, and just the right size to fit the opening when the front half of the roof is raised. One of these frames is covered with muslin and the other with wire netting. In fine weather both sides of the front portion of the roof are opened, and on very cold days the side over the muslin. These frames are made to slide. In feeding and caring for the fowls one frame is slid over the other, and both are removed when cleaning the second floor after the fowls have been driven down stairs.

In making the nests, a ten-inch board, two feet four inches long is placed in the opposite end from the window, fourteen inches from the end; two pieces of board fourteen inches long and three inches wide are used to divide the two nests and hold the straw in place where the hens enter.

The wide board is eight inches shorter than the width of the coop, and is fastened to the front side of the coop, leaving an eight by ten inch space at the back side for the hens to enter the nests, which are under the roost boards.

A board fourteen inches wide by three feet long is placed over the nests with a two-inch strip around the sides, and a roost one by two inches and three feet long is fastened in position in the center of the board three inches above it. The roost is used for a handle to remove the dropping board when gathering the eggs or to clean the board, which should be a portion of the day's work.

A strip of board four inches wide is placed at the window end of the coop next to the stairs to prevent the litter from being scratched down stairs.

Frames are made of 7-8x1 inch strips of lumber and covered with one-inch wire netting to enclose the two sides of the lower story. Two short strips an inch square and 4 in. long are nailed to the foundation about 4 in. from each end. The frames are hinged to these strips, and a round spring window catch, to hold the frame in position when closed, is put through the top strip of the frame. The frames are lowered when spading or raking the soil. They are made enough smaller than the opening so that they will not bind.

A frame is made of two-by-fours six feet long and three feet wide. They are set edgewise and are used as sills. Place them where you wish the coop to stand, and level them, with the top about two inches above the ground, leaving a two-inch space to be filled with fine gravel and sand. The coop is placed on these sills, and faces the south in winter and north in summer.

The door on the back side of the first floor of the coop is never opened in winter, and the front side is opened on pleasant days. By opening both sides and the front half of the roof in summer, a shade is provided by the hanging doors and roof, admitting a free circulation of air to keep the fowls comfortable, and in fine condition.

As these coops are all made from panels they may be constructed indoors, and but a few minutes will be required to set them up when completed.

Twelve-feet lumber either six or twelve inches wide is used without waste and with but little ripping the boards.

Or if it is desired, one of the long sash described in connection with the other coops may be used in the upper side of the floor that encloses the lower part. If used, the upper outer edge may be beveled so that it is only as thick as the board above it, to shed water, and the hinges let in as far as necessary so that the inside will be flush to allow the door to close. This will furnish an abundance of light in cold and stormy weather, when the lower part must be closed.

Double Winter Colony Coop—The Roof and Sides are Adjusted for the Warmest Weather, Giving Perfect Ventilation and Shade. The Center Section of the Roof is Stationary

DOUBLE WINTER COLONY COOP.

We hardly expect farmers to build many of the single winter colony coops on account of the small number of birds they afford protection for and the additional amount of labor required in caring for a number of small flocks, in place of the one large one generally kept on the farm. However, should they try several small flocks in place of the one large one, it would not require many seasons to show them the advantages to be gained and the increased egg production derived by the use of the colony system.

Our double house is designed largely for this class of poultry keepers, as well as for others who have but little time to care for fowls, and for those living in very cold sections. With birds having large combs the double coop has advantages. The birds are warmer in this coop, yet they have all the advantages of the single coop, excepting that the flock is double the size. There are twice the number of birds in the coop, and the natural heat would be twice as great; besides they are more than twice the distance from the muslin window in the end, making the loss from radiation very much less than where the birds roost within a few feet of the window.

THE NEW ECONOMY COOP FOR WINTER AND SUMMER USE.

During the past two years while raising so many fowls on our small city yard we have been forced many times to keep more fowls in the coops than is best and have often kept the pullets in the brooder coops until they matured and commenced laying. When the weather grew cold in the fall, it was necessary to close the coops at night making it too low for the fully matured fowls so they did not have head room in the brooder coops. It was then necessary to double them up by removing the top of one and setting another one on top of it to make the coop about two feet high. These we used for keeping odd lots of cockerels not used in our breeding pens, and pullets not likely to commence laying very soon, and we have been surprised to note the condition of the fowls thus kept and how early the pullets commenced laying, and also how well they continued to lay while thus confined. We also learned that the fowls in three of these coops could be cared for in about the same length of time required to care for those in one of the Winter Colony Coops. This, of course, would not matter much where there were but few fowls, but where a great many of them are kept, the saving of a little time in caring

The Foundation of the Coop and the Roost Board in the Hand of a Practical Poultry Keeper

for each coop is a matter worthy our consideration. One of the objections to our system of housing the laying stock has been in the amount of labor necessary in looking after so many coops, and the cost of building our regular Winter Colony Coop. We hardly think it possible at the present time to construct any kind of house or coop that will bring about as desirable conditions for the poultry at all seasons of the year, and at the same cost and outlay for material and labor as in the new coop.

Before giving the plans to our readers, we have experimented in building several different styles, until we are pretty well convinced that the one we now have is superior in many respects to anything we have formerly produced. Our efforts have been largely to economize along all lines, and for this purpose have tried to construct all of our coops without glass, and several coops were made and used without any glass making it necessary to leave the roof slightly raised that the fowls might get light through the muslin covered sliding frame. When driving storms came we were annoyed by the rain blowing under the cover,

The Nest is Placed in the Back Center of the Floor End Coop, and is Fastened Near the Top, Giving the Hens the Floor Room Under It

and snow drifting in during the day when it was necessary to give the fowls light. Of course on cold, stormy nights the coops are always completely closed and the storm is kept out.

Mr. Cox discovered that a small light of glass in front of his brooder coop would be an advantage, so the top might be completely closed during severe storms, and we could at once see that it would be a decided advantage in our deep coops, and we are now making them with the sash six feet long and one foot wide to take the place of the front board on the upper section of the coop.

We find it an advantage to make a foundation to set these coops on where the ground is wet, and raise the ground in one end of the foundation two or three inches above the level of the ground outside of the coop. The foundation can be made of inexpensive lumber and when used will save the bottom edges of the coop from decaying, making the cost less to keep the coops in the best condition after being used many years.

After Cleaning the Roost in the Morning it is Turned Up Edgewise Against the Back of the Coop

CONSTRUCTION:—The foundation frames are made of 1x4in. lumber just the size of the coop, six feet long and three feet wide outside with a four-inch partition in the center. In one end of the coop the floor is laid on strips about one and one-half inches from the bottom to keep the boards off the ground and prevent them from getting damp. The floor is then covered with one-ply roofing material that the moisture from the top may not penetrate the boards when the litter becomes damp.

The coops and foundations were formerly made of square edged boards. We are now making them ship lapped to hold the sections and foundation together without being nailed and to

Economy Coop

76

prevent the storms and wind from going through the open cracks which are likely to appear when square edged boards are used. Any lumber dealer understands the term ship lap so that you will not have any trouble in getting this kind of lumber. The next section of the box which rests on the foundation is made from lumber twelve inches wide and is just the right size to fit the

The Roost Board is Dropped at Night as Shown in the Illustration

foundation. The top section is also made from the same width lumber (twelve inches wide) and just fits on the under section making the coop three feet wide by six feet long and twenty-four inches deep. The end boards of the top section are ten and three-fourths inches wide or one and one-fourth inches narrower than the front and back of the coop, to allow room for the sliding frame and about three-eighths inch space between theframe and roof for ventilation through the muslin curtain when the roof is closed. A sash one foot wide by six feet long, having six panes of glass is used to form the front of the coop, and the bottom of the sash is also rabbeted to fit the foundation. Parting strips 1-2x7-8 in., which are used in building window frames, may be had at almost any lumber yard. These are nailed lengthwise on the inside of the back board and the inside top edge of the sash t 1-4 in. down from the top so that they will just come level with the ends of the coop for the muslin frame to slide on.

SLIDING FRAME:—The muslin frame is made of 7-8x1-2 in. strips of lumber mitered at the corners and with a center piece of the same material to strengthen the long sides. The frame is then covered with one-inch wire netting and over this is tacked an inexpensive grade of unbleached muslin. The entire frame is covered for cold weather, or where the climate is cold, but during the warm weather only one-half of the frame is covered with muslin. This frame may be made of 1-2x1 1-2 or 2-in. strips and lapped at the corners instead of mitering, which might be easier for some people who are not accustomed to this kind of work.

We are now putting the Paroid on top of the frame work instead of on the under side, with three strips on top as described below.

In making the roof two strips 6 ft. 2 in. long are used, the front one 3 in. wide, and the back one 2 in. For the ribs on the under side we use eight strips 2 ft. 9 in. long and 2 in. wide, and one strip 2 ft. 9 in. long and 3 in. wide. For the top we use two strips 3 ft. 2 in. long and 2 in. wide, and one strip 3 ft. 2 in. long and 3 in. wide. All these are 7-8 in. thick.

The Paroid is 3 ft. wide and we cut two pieces 3 ft. 2 in. long. The ends of each piece of Paroid are nailed to the long strips with the outer edge of each piece even with the ends of the long strips. This makes the roof 6 ft. 2 in. long and 3 ft. 2 in. wide, with a 2 in. open space in the center between the two pieces of Paroid.

Now turn the roof over and nail the nine 2 ft. 9 in. strips, the 3 in. one in the center, between the inside edges of the long strips. These shorter strips should be cut so as to crowd the long strips apart and stretch the Paroid to remove all wrinkles. When these strips are all nailed in their places, turn the roof over again and nail the Paroid to these short strips, taking pains to see that the inside edges are securely fastened to the 3 in. strip. Fill the space between the edges with roofing cement or paint, and also let it come over a little on each edge. You now have left the three 3 ft. 2 in. strips; nail the 3 in. strip over this center space, and a 2 in. strip at each end. This will now be the top of the roof, with three strips showing over the Paroid, while the under side will have the two long strips and nine short ones. This arrangement makes the roof absolutely waterproof.

A strip of wood 1-2 in. thick by 1 1-2 in. wide and 3 ft. long is used to hold the roof in any desired position. A small hole is bored through one end of the stick to fasten it to the top edge of the front sash. The hole should be large enough to allow the stick to move at any angle without binding but not so large that it will slide off the head of the screw. Several larger holes are bored in the stick so that they will slide over the head of the screw in the center of the front edge of the roof that it may be adjusted at any desired angle, as it is sometimes advisable to change the adjustment in varied weather conditions. When the sun shines, the roof should be wide open, and when it is stormy, it should be nearly closed, but not entirely closed unless the weather is very cold.

In making the roost board a frame 15 in. wide and 2 ft. 10 in. long is made of 7-8 x 1 1-2 in. strips. Roofing material is nailed to the bottom of this frame which makes it very light and easily cleaned. Two small blocks, 1 1-2 in. wide and 4 in. long are nailed on the top edge of the ends of the frame. A strip of wood for the roost, 7-8 in. thick and 2 in. wide, with the corners slightly rounded, is nailed on these blocks. We formerly placed this roost board across one end of the coop, but after using the sash in the front of the coop it would make it rather cold for the hens roosting on the end next to the window. The roost is now being placed against the back side and in the end without the floor. The center board, 8 ins. wide, is set edgewise on the center board of the foundation and is held in place with cleats nailed to the inside of the coop. The board is to prevent the hens from scratching the straw into the end without the floor. Small cleats are nailed horizontally to this center board and also in the end of the coop 15 ins. down from the top to support the roost board, and during the day the roost may be turned up edgewise against the back of the coop to make more room.

The nest is used in one corner of the coop at the top and is made 12 in. wide, 16 in. long and 10 in. deep. The bottom board is 24 ins. long to provide a lighting place for the hens in entering the nest. The coops should face the south during the winter and north in the summer.

In the construction of three of our coops in the illustration eight-ounce duck cloth is used in place of lumber. It is tacked both on the inside and outside of light wood frames allowing an air space of nearly an inch. We are not sure that more than one thickness is required even where the temperature drops many degrees below zero. Where the weather is warmer the coop would answer every purpose when covered with muslin or cotton cloth, and when only one thickness of the cloth is used in covering the sides of the coop the sash in front would be a very small item.

CARE OF THE FOWLS:—Oat straw is used in the floor end of the coop about four inches deep and during damp weather it is necessary to change the straw twice each week, although it is generally in good condition for a week during the winter and two weeks during the summer.

The first thing in the morning a little wheat or buckwheat is sprinkled in the straw, after being sure that there is not any left over from feeding the day before. The droppings on the roost boards are emptied into a bushel basket and the roosts turned up edgewise out of the way against the back of the coop. The water troughs are then rinsed and filled. A handful of oats is spaded in the dirt end of the coop and all straw and rubbish scratched over the center board are removed. Sprouted oats are then fed. A warm mash is used for the noon feed, consisting of equal parts by measure, of wheat bran, ground oats (hull and all), and corn meal, and as much cut alfalfa or clover as the fowls can be induced to eat. We are now using it so that it constitutes one-half the bulk of the mash. One tablespoonful of salt and a teaspoonful of black pepper is used in a half bushel of feed. Boiling water is used to moisten the mash, and after it is thoroughly mixed it is covered for a half hour or more to steam and swell before feeding. One pint of good beef scraps may be added to a half bushel of feed, although good results may be had without them. It is possible to get very good results without the warm mash by keeping wheat bran, and cut clover in the hoppers. It is best to keep each kind of food in separate hoppers that the fowls may make their own choice in balancing their ration. About one hour before dark, cracked corn and wheat or buckwheat, is thrown in the straw when there is not any left from the morning feeding. The roosts are then dropped in place and the eggs gathered.

When these coops are used and this system of care and feeding is employed, the eggs will surely pay for the feed and labor, besides leaving a good balance for profit. We have one pen of White Leghorns, seven hens and a cockerel, that have produced eggs enough, at an average price of 30 cents a dozen, to yield a profit of nearly three dollars per hen in seven months, from December to July.

WINTER QUARTERS.

The climatic conditions differ to such an extent that it is a difficult proposition to formulate definite plans that would be best adapted to all localities. The foremost thought in planning should be to arrange the winter quarters for the comfort of the fowls, although this is generally a secondary matter and the tatendant's comfort and ease in handling the poultry is often the first to be considered. This, of course should not be ignored when it is possible to combine comfort for both the poultry and the keeper; and right here I wish to make the statement that women are often the most successful poultry keepers, for the reason that they look more to the comfort of the fowls than does the average man.

It matters not what the breed or what the feed may be; when comfortable quarters are not provided, the results will not be satisfactory. Even though wishing to follow our system of keeping poultry, it is not positively essential that the old poultry houses be discarded and a lot of our system coops arranged to take their place in which to winter the poultry. The winter house is, in fact, the least important in our new way of keeping poultry so long as the flocks are small and the coops comfortable. It is a fact, however, that when poultry have access to the finely sifted ground in at least a small section of the coops the results will be more satisfactory than when they are confined over a cement or board floor and do not have access to the ground, and the eggs will be of better quality from which to produce strong chickens. While the ground is an advantage it is not an absolute necessity to get good results. The upper story of a building may be utilized for winter quarters when such rooms are already on a place where one's space and capital are limited.

Comfort for the fowls means as much sunshine as it is possible to get, no dampness, and fresh air from muslin or open windows when the weather conditions will permit, even though very cold.

The size and shape of the glass windows and other openings to be covered with muslin are of the greatest importance and seldom get the proper consideration. The windows should be the long way up and down instead of being placed in a horizontal position, that the rays of the sun may reach every foot of floor space sometime during the day, and to get these results it is necessary that the window openings be nearly full length between the sill and plate.

When the house has but one slant to the roof, the high side should face the south, when the windows can be placed in the south side of the building. If the windows are to be placed in the east side, the front or high side of the building should face the east, as the rays of the sun will then reach a greater depth, or farther back in the room than when the windows are placed under the eaves or on the low side of the building.

A great many houses have been built with the low side facing the south, the builder thinking that the sun shining directly against the roof would furnish more heat. There is always plenty of heat when the sun shines, and the sun is of greater value when shining in the building than on the broad side of the roof.

The greater the depth of the building, the larger the windows and muslin openings should be, that the rear of the room may be lighted on the darkest days. When the room is 6 ft. wide by 6 ft. deep it should be provided with a window having six panes of 9 x 12 glass, and a room 6 ft. wide by 12 ft. deep should have a window with twelve panes of 9 x 12 glass, and twenty-four panes the same size are not too many when the room is 12 ft. wide by 12 ft. deep, in order that the hens may readily find the small kernels of grain in the deep litter on the darkest days. The size 9x12 is given as a basis from which to estimate the correct amount of glass and muslin for any size room.

The opening for the ventilation should be practically the same size as the window and a light wood frame covered with a coarse grade of unbleached muslin made to close the opening on very cold or stormy days and at night.

Ten hens in a pen 6 x 6 ft., having six panes of 9 x 12 glass, should give good results, and when the pens are larger, one hen to a pane of glass is all that should be allowed, and they should never exceed the limit of the room 12 x 12 ft., having twenty-four panes of glass, 9 x 12, and twenty-four hens.

It will not require as much labor to care for a given number of hens when in large flocks, but to get the very best results, six hens should be the limit of the number kept in a single pen.

The opening should always be on the south side of the house when it is possible. There are many poultry houses and barns already built which could be adapted to the business, and it is not always possible to get the opening on the south side on account of their location or, possibly, by their joining other buildings on the south.

Our next choice would be the east side for the opening, that the fowls may get the early morning sun, and when it is possible to arrange openings on both the east and west sides, the most desirable conditions may be had by opening the east side during the forenoon and the west side during the afternoon. When thus planned it will be necessary to arrange close fitting doors that when one side is closed and the other open there will not be any cracks through which to create a draught. This plan also has the advantage of making it possible to open the side of the building on which the wind is not blowing, on cloudy days.

When the openings are on two sides as above, the roosting boxes or bed rooms should be placed about in the center of the room on the south side, and when the opening is on the south side of the building the boxes should be placed directly opposite on the north side of the room. The roosting boxes should be just large enough to accommodate the fowls, allowing room for the long tails of the male birds and just room enough to allow the fowls to stand on the perches without hitting their heads against the ceiling of the boxes.

The perches should be about three inches from the bottom of the boxes to prevent the fluff feathers from being soiled. The front is the only opening of the roosting boxes, but this should be closed with a curtain made of a coarse grade of muslin tacked along the top edge of the box and arranged to hang close at the bottom and sides.

By providing a run-way to the roosting boxes with an entrance at one end of the lower corner, the muslin curtain may be gradually closed, as the fowls become acquainted with the new roosting quarters, until it is all hooked down leaving but one corner loose. The fowls will soon learn the door-way and will enter the box at night and leave it in the early morning without attention. The boxes should be cleaned every day.

Dry, clean litter is of the greatest importance and the fowls seem to get the most comfort when scratching for small particles of food, and are nearly covered in the litter. Oat straw is as good as any material and can be obtained in small bales in nearly all localities. Although this is not especially of any great food value, it is surprising to see how much of it will be eaten by the fowls even though they are provided with cut clover, sprouted oats and other green food. It is not generally understood how much bulky food is required and when this is not provided they will often greedily devour feathers longer than one's finger, which is no doubt one of the reasons for feather pulling.

The yearly cry of infertile eggs is more often due to a lack of coarse food than to any other cause.

If looking for a sight that will do your heart good, just throw a handful of finely chopped, cooked lean beef in a thick covering of oat straw. The straw will not only fly, but the music made by the hens will do one good who is a lover of the music furnished by a healthy flock. This is one kind of music that pays, and pays well, as the singing hen is sure to be productive and make its owner feel like singing even though unable to "pitch a tune."

We have taken up the matter quite fully regarding comfortable winter quarters, and we do not wish to be misunderstood, leaving an impression that winter chickens can as well be raised in buildings as in brooder coops placed out of doors. Raising chickens is a decidedly different proposition from that of keeping them after they have been raised, and when the best success is to be had it will be necessary to raise the chickens on the ground in a regular brooder coop.

We would not think of keeping more than fifteen hens in a pen and six hens will do better. Where the climate is very cold we would not allow over four square feet floor space to a hen, but in warmer localities, where the temperature seldom reaches zero, it is best to allow each hen a floor space of five or six square feet.

The ceiling of the room should not be higher than is required to give the keeper head-room when caring for the fowls. When necessary to economize in the remodeling, strips of wood or poles may be strung across the ceiling and thickly covered with straw or other inexpensive material. Several thicknesses of burlap sacking tacked to the under side of the strips of boards will also make a desirable ceiling, and when this is used the straw would not be required unless where the fowls to be wintered have large combs and it is desirable to make the coop as warm as possible.

We have great success in raising poultry in our small coops, three feet by six feet. The young chicks are kept at first in the low brooder coop, one foot high; when they outgrow this, they are placed in the Ecomony coop, which affords ample space for them as long as they are kept for breeders.

The low coop can be converted into the higher one by adding a twelve inch section between the foundation and the one with the sash, and to which the roof is attached.

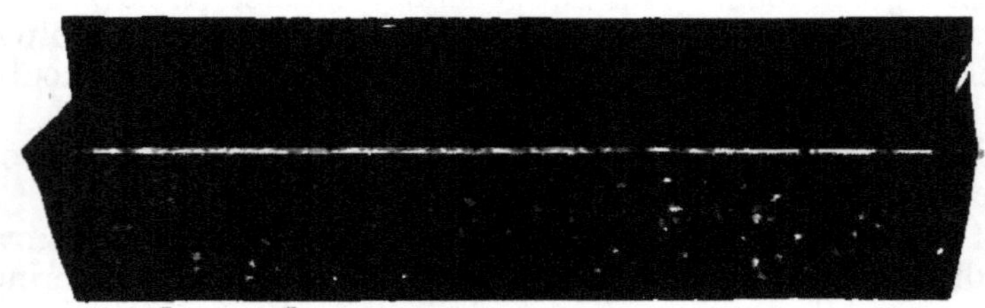

GALVANIZED IRON TROUGH.

The galvanized iron trough shown in the illustration is well adapted to our colony coops, and is used either for food or water. The illustration shows the construction. The size we generally use is three and one-half inches deep, and two and one-half inches across the opening and fifteen inches long. The top edge is turned back, forming a groove which is hooked over special nails with large heads, so that the trough may be placed without looking for the nails or holes.

Ice is easily removed by springing the sides, and the trough will expand rather than crack when the water is freezing.

By giving the ends a half-inch bevel, making the bottom one inch shorter than the top, they may be nested, and will take less room when stored.

SPROUTING OATS

Green Food Costing About 15 Cents Per Bushel.

This food has proved itself to be for us a most excellent egg-producer. It serves as a green food all the year around, and the fowls are extremely fond of it. The way this food is prepared is as follows:

Take a quantity of oats or rye and soak them in water for twelve hours. Then pour off the water and put the oats in an ordinary box which has holes in the bottom and let the water drain off. The oats are watered with a sprinkling pot night and morning and are stirred with a stick or hand, before watering. As soon as the oats begin to sprout we spread them out in a box to the thickness of about an inch, and still continue to water them night and morning, but do not stir them after they begin to sprout. In about ten days or two weeks, depending upon how warm the room is in which they are kept, they will be ready to feed. When in the proper condition to feed, the sod will be about two inches thick, and the growth of green feed on top will be about one or two inches high. We feed a block about two or three inches square of this to each pen of six fowls. We have been using this feed throughout the winter and must say that our hens never laid so well. We have averaged a fifty per cent. egg production all winter long. This can also be fed to young chicks, although it should be fed at a time when the sprouts are just starting, or they should be cut fine.

OVER $1,000 FROM POULTRY AND EGGS PRODUCED FROM SIXTY BREEDING HENS IN EIGHT MONTHS ON A CITY LOT FORTY FEET SQUARE.

Under several headings in this book we give particulars about our work this season that has brought such large returns from sixty hens on a space forty feet square in our city garden. While these figures are the result of our labor for several months less than a year, it has taken us six years to build up the strain of fowls from which this record was made. With our present knowledge of breeding as set forth in this book we think a better record could be made in a shorter space of time.

By having our little plant on a prominent street in the city we had free advertising, and it proved to be of the very best kind. Parties passing could hardly help seeing a beautiful lot of pure white fowls nicely kept, and those who were familiar with poultry could readily see that they were well bred.

We commenced setting the Cycle Brooder Hatcher, or Metal Mother, on the 10th of December, 1907, so that the first chickens would hatch on the first of January. Another lot was set a week later to get some baby chickens to exhibit in the Elmira Poultry Show.

The baby chickens were brooded in the Metal Mother the first week, and eggs were being incubated in the same machine constantly from December until the present time, keeping a supply of newly-hatched baby chickens in a glass case where they could be seen by people passing by. It was not long before there was such a demand for the eggs at $5 per sitting that all we could spare were soon engaged.

These early chickens were also hatched to test the brooders without heat during the coldest weather, and the results were very much better than we had ever had before with winter chickens. On account of the winter hatching during a few previous years, our hens were more productive during the three winter months than at any other time of the year, and one of the greatest mistakes we ever made was in selling over a thousand eggs for table use when they should have been incubated. It would have been an easy matter to raise at least 500 chickens from the eggs sold for table use, and the early chickens would have brought more cash than we have received from all other sales. It would have been necessary to increase the size of the plant during the time of raising the chickens, and that would have been an easy matter as the garden at that time was not in use and would have been improved if covered with coops until planting time.

It is now nearly the first of September and we are still setting all the eggs not sold for hatching and will continue to do so all through the winter that we may get the full value of every egg laid by our hens, and will make an effort to double the returns the coming year from our small city plant.

During the eight months, beginning January 1st, 1908, we made the following cash sales of eggs, chickens and poultry, all of which have been produced on one small lot less than 40 feet square:

Broilers and table eggs.	$ 149.00
Eggs for hatching.	349.00
Baby chickens fresh from the hatcher.	283.00
Hens, pullets and cockerels for breeding.	275.00
	$1056.00

We have on hand about 200 head of chickens, from those just hatched to fully matured, more than we had at the beginning of the year, and when they are sold the net profit from this very small poultry plant will exceed $1,500.00 in one year.

While the space of ground occupied by the poultry has been given as forty feet square, one corner of this space had a small building on it not used for poultry where fifty or more chickens could have been raised, adding considerable to the returns from the small plot of ground.

On account of the great amount of business we have had during the year the poultry work has often been neglected, and the chickens and poultry allowed to suffer. We hope to do better the coming year and give the poultry better care, that we may learn just how many dollars worth of poultry it is possible to raise on a square foot of ground in one year.

We now have grape vines set between the coops to furnish shade, and when they come into full bearing will add many dollars to the income of the plant.

There were always eggs with imperfect shells that were not suitable for hatching, supplying the table for a family of five. One to three chickens have been used on the table nearly every week, no account of which is given in this report.

HOW POULTRY HELPS TO MAKE A GOOD GARDEN.

In estimating the value of poultry products the real value of the fertilizer produced is too often lost sight of. Comparing its value with that of the commercial fertilizers it would be perfectly safe to credit the poultry business with at least one-fourth the total amount of the feed bill and especially when one has land enough to use it to the best advantage in growing small fruit or other graden truck.

From the recent tests we have made of its use we hardly think its true value is correctly estimated. Like our intensive system of poultry culture, wonderful results may be had from a very small space of ground by using it much more liberally than has been considered advisable. It is a fact that too liberal a use at an improper time will kill almost any kind of vegetation, but with proper application fully one-fifth in bulk may be mixed with the average soil, producing surprising results.

About the middle of June, or too late in the spring, as stated by a florist, to grow Cannas to perfection, we thought a nice bed in our front yard would improve its looks, and we started out with a determined effort to kill or cure as the case might be. Three bushels of fertilizer which had been emptied in the garden previous to several heavy rain storms was mixed with three times its bulk of garden soil. This was placed where the plants were to be set, at a depth of ten inches. About two months after the plants were set some of them were over six feet tall and have continued to grow since the photograph was taken.

When extremely large quantities of the fertilizer are to be used it should be thoroughly mixed with the soil and subjected to several rain storms, before planting time, or placed where the heating properties will be destroyed before it is to be used.

We now keep large piles mixed with garden soil and sifted for immediate use so that any kind of plants may be set at any time.

Grape vines were set in rows running north and south and the rows about eight feet apart to furnish shade during the extreme heat of the summer. They were set one year ago last spring and the Summer Colony Coops were placed close to the roots of the vines. Quantities of the fertilizer have been spaded into the ground almost daily. In addition to this they were banked with a very rich mixture to a depth of about ten inches as a protection to the roots; however, after one year's growth the vines were photographed showing their condition and the abundance of fruit they are carrying as the result of a single season's growth.

One hundred strawberry plants were set in rows about six

Roses Picked in August

feet apart. Large quantities of unadulterated fertilizer were placed between the rows which would have covered the entire plot of ground, and the fertilizer was gradually worked into the soil around the plants, producing remarkable growth of plants and heavy fruiting this season.

Several varieties of roses were treated in a like manner giving us a constant supply of roses for table bouquets all through the dry summer months. The cut given in connection with this article was made from a photograph taken from roses picked from our bushes the latter part of August.

Tender broilers, eggs, fruit, vegetables and roses fresh from the garden as often as desired is a luxury not enjoyed by many people. By adopting the intensive culture and making every available foot of ground produce something of value, nearly everyone could enjoy at least a portion of the good things and of better quality than could be procured from the market.

HOW TO MAKE A LIVING FROM POULTRY.

This is, without doubt, the one question uppermost in the minds of many of our readers, and to answer it intelligently is by no means a small undertaking. However, we know for a fact that there is a living in keeping poultry and a better living than ninety-nine out of every hundred who seek work for a living are making.

It is far from a "get rich quick" scheme, and can only succeed with almost constant care and deep study that no little detail may be neglected and a positive knowledge at all times that every last chicken or hen in the flock is not suffering from neglect.

An educated eye to take in the true condition of the birds at a glance is of more value to the poultry keeper than the unlimited use of money, if the keeper profits by what is seen and does the necessary work at once to improve the conditions. "Tomorrow" will *never* answer in a successful poultry business.

In ninety-nine cases of failure in any business the cause may be traced to the lack of attention to business at the proper time, or to giving more thought to the things not concerning the business and unless one is willing to devote almost the entire time and thought to the many little things so important to success, the chances are against the living from poultry. It is also the one business where brains count for more than muscle, as the muscle can be purchased at a moderate price, but the brains must accompany the living.

It is very nice and also a shorter road to the living to be able to purchase valuable birds that are worth the price, still it is not a necessary requisite to the best success. All breeders, even the most successful, find their most difficult task to be the keeping their young chickens alive, and when one is successful in raising them there will be more to bank on for the living than in being able to find a market for that which they cannot raise.

We get hundreds of letters telling of some particular location and asking advice regarding the possibilities for them in the poultry business there and our answer would be nearly the same to all, as the location is but a small factor in the development of a poultry business, provided that the ground is dry, or that it could be drained. Many places are naturally fitted and could be turned into a poultry yard with but little work and expense.

In asking our advice as to the possibilities in any particular case we could give a more accurate answer if we knew the person who would have charge of the poultry than we could by having a full description of the land and buildings where the business is to be handled.

One should possess an unusual amount of stick-to-itiveness and have a determined mind to win at the chosen occupation. All other things must, and will, come by degrees, and a successful plant may be established in a very short time when the proper push is behind the enterprise.

After being satisfied that one is qualified for the business and is willing to work for the living just as would be necessary when employed by another, the work of raising the chickens to perfection should be the first one to master, as it is the foundation of the poultry business.

Fully three-fourths of the the poultry that will soon go into winter quarters will be too old to be profitable, and in nearly every case it is on account of not having been able to raise the chickens, and in many instances they have been carelessly lost from neglect.

At the present stage of poultry keeping there is no excuse for allowing dogs, cats or hawks to carry the young chickens off, any more than a successful merchant would leave the door of his store unlocked thinking that possibly by some good luck the goods would always be found in the place. At least ninety per cent. of the chickens hatched should be raised to maturity and unless this can be accomplished year in and year out, there is something faulty about the care or system, which should be changed or corrected.

The one in charge of the poultry plant is the greatest factor in making the business a success. If determined to win and work along some definite line, success will be sure.

I have always been considered visionary, and the longer I live the more need there seems for one to be visionary if there is to be anything gained in life more than a living. We must set our stakes high, then drive hard to the mark until the goal for which we are aiming has been reached.

There is a good living in poultry by just keeping ordinary thoroughbred stock. Still greater success may be had when the best quality is kept, and they should be improved each year. The demand for poultry of the finest quality is always in excess of the supply, and when one has some extra good ones to sell the profits are greatly increased and there is an incentive for one to aim still higher. As a basis for estimating profits for the production of market eggs we will take for granted that the average hen with the average care will produce 150 eggs in a year, and that it will cost as much to raise the hen as she will bring after completing the year's work of producing eggs. The difference, then, between the cost of feed consumed and the amount the eggs will bring would be all profit (or pay for labor when the owner is doing the work).

The average market price for eggs is twenty-four cents a dozen, making the net proceeds from the hen during the year $3.00. At the present high price for feed and grain it will cost $1.50 to supply a 150-egg hen 365 days, leaving a net profit of $1.50 a year. One good, active person can care tor 1,000 laying hens which would yield a profit of $1,500.00, when the care given the entire lot would be equal to the care given a single flock of six hens in a pen.

It now costs $1.85 a year to keep a 200-egg hen, making the per cent. profit greater than when the 150-egg hen is kept, at a cost of $1.50 a year, and the difference between the 150-egg hen and the 200-egg hen is largely in the breeding, although the care given them has about as much to do with a large egg yield as the breeding. $1,500.00 a year would be considered quite a snug little income by the average person and is more than the average person would make, for the simple reason that they do not think it possible to get such returns and are afraid to set their stakes for fear of failure, which only comes to those who are looking for it, just as the greatest success comes to one who dreams dreams and sees visions and then uses the talent given to carry on the work as planned, in the most practical and business-like manner.

At the average market price of eggs the net price from 600 laying hens, kept in flocks of six hens each, at the Australian laying contest, has been $3.37 a hen, and the amount is increasing each year, as the store of knowledge of the keeper is increasing and the poultry improved to make every move count for more eggs.

The most common cause of failure in the poultry business is

without doubt, from inattention and its being handled as a side issue, the fowls getting but a remnant of thought and attention after one is exhausted by close attention to other business and has nothing left for the sadly neglected poultry. Give the poultry the same careful study and care it is necessary to give any other remunerative business and there will not be any question as to which will pay the best.

NEW AND BETTER FACILITIES.

We have purchased thirty acres of land in this city, about one mile from our present location for the purpose of conducting a poultry school and experimental poultry plant. The land is nicely situated, being between two direct lines of street cars and is also easy of access to three of the principal railroads of the city. There are about twelve to fifteen acres of high, gravelly ground, slightly rolling, and a portion of this ground has a gradual slope to the south. This part will be used for our poultry plant. The balance of the ground is low and not available in the present condition for poultry culture, but this will not matteras we shall only devote a portion of the ground at first to our poultry work. We shall use several hundred coops, about half of them for mature fowls, and the others for chickens of various ages. From each breeding pen of five hens and one cock we can raise from 100 to 200 chicks each year, and in this way can increase the flock to almost any extent, and at the same time furnish several thousands of young chicks and growing fowls for breeding purposes.

In addition to the poultry that will be kept on the two acres there will be grape vines, plum and cherry trees and sun flowers to furnish shade during the summer. The hens will make the vines, trees and sunflowers productive and at the same time they will be greatly benefitted during the hot summer months by being protected from the direct rays of the sun.

This article, we trust, will serve a double purpose, by giving our readers a thorough understanding of the work we are undertaking, viz:

1.—The possibility of a large poultry business on two acres of ground.

2.—The excellent opportunities offered anyone who would like thoroughly to master all branches of poultry work, and the practical plan for others to follow to get larger returns from a small plot of ground than can be had in almost any other way.

The portion of the farm devoted to poultry culture is slightly raised, the north side being about four feet higher than the south

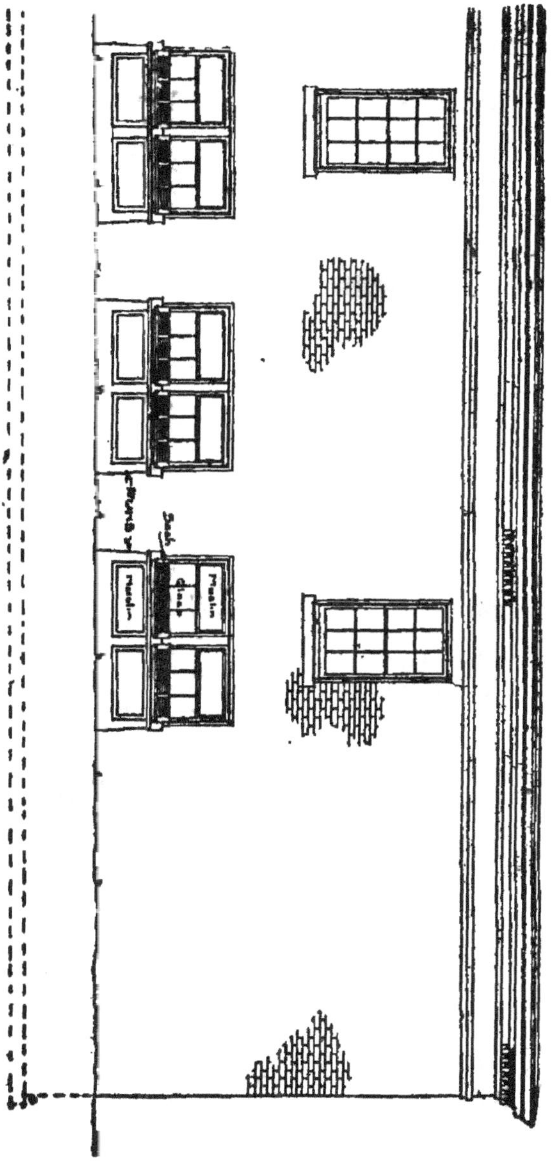

ELEVATION

Plan of the Hatcher and Brooder House

which is four hundred feet distant The soil is never muddy, being composed of sand, gravel, loam and cobble-stones, and the ground can be walked over any season of the year without soiling more than the soles of one's shoes. The natural conditions are the very best with the exception of the stones which can be screened out at any time, although this will require a great amount of labor, but will be labor well spent when the work is finally completed.

The soil must be fine and mellow to induce the fowls to scratch in searching for grain buried beneath the surface.

During the winter the coops are open to the south to catch every ray of sunshine and in the summer they face the north, the roof acting as a shade board, and four sun flowers planted south of each coop help to shade the fowls from the piercing sun during the warmest days.

Even though a thousand acres are given a flock, better conditions can not be had for growing chickens to perfection or for getting the largest yields from laying hens.

A long concrete feed and supply building with an incubator cellar is placed at the south end of the poultry plant, and the feed and supplies will be easily accessible so that the work may be handled with the greatest ease. The incubator cellar will be provided with one hundred hatchers for the use of the students.

Four months of the year oats will be sprouted in the cellar to supply the fowls with green food in addition to the alfalfa or dry clover clippings which will be fed liberally in the moist mash at noon.

To produce the best quality of clover clippings a two acre lawn seeded with White Dutch clover will be cut with a lawn mower every week and the clippings spread out two inches deep under cover to dry, and before making the second cutting, the first lot will be ready to sack and store away for the winter supply to be fed during the months of December, January, February and Mar h.

The farm will be used for educational and experimental purposes and will be made to pay a larger profit than one would think possible. Raising chickens and compelling the hens to be productive is no longer an experiment with the writer, and if permitted to retain his health and carry on the work outlined, there will not be any question as to the final outcome of the enterprise. There is yet much to be learned about keeping poultry, and with the advantages of the farm, of improved breeding stock and of the increased facilities we shall have for conducting the experiments, we hope to give our readers the results of many valuable lessons learned during the year and for many years to come.

We furnish on another page the plan for our new hatcher and

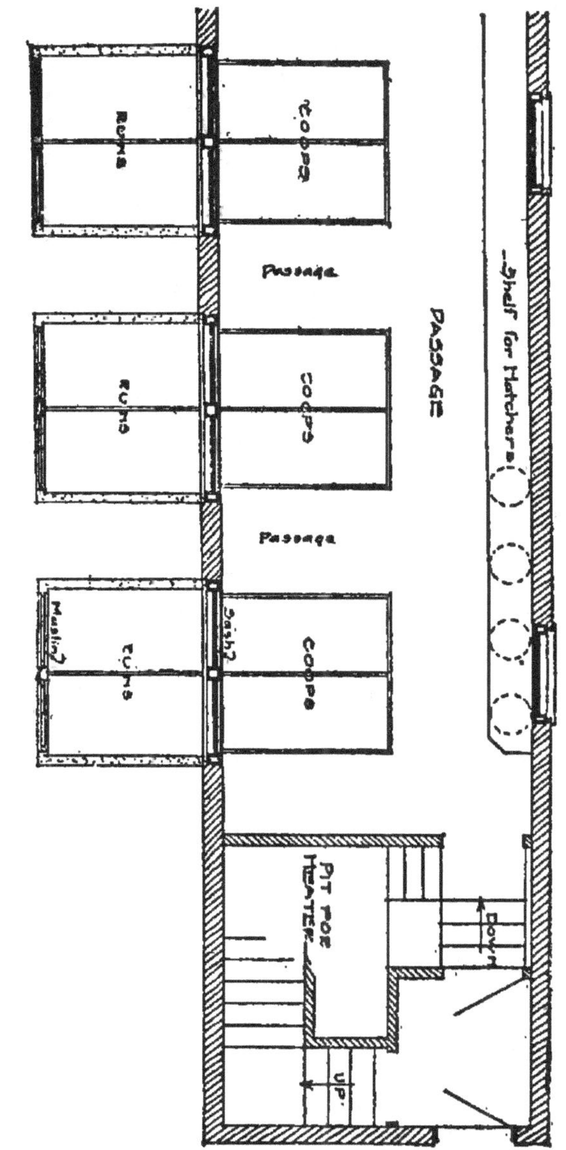

Section of the Hatcher and Brooder House

brooder house now in use at the farm. The building has been planned to serve instruction purposes, and to take care of the chicks from the time they are hatched until well past the danger point. Everything has been laid out so as to facilitate the work, and we feel that this arrangement will better suit our purpose than anything we have ever tried when handling chicks in large numbers. It will be noted that it is the intention to start the chicks inside in a heated building. It has been thought best to follow this plan for, in the school work the brooders must be opened frequently for inspection and demonstration, and this condition is very hard on the chicks in cold weather, and it is somewhat easier to feed and care for them on stormy days, although we are sure that without any heat at all we get chicks of greater vitality.

The building is approximately 12 by 106 feet, two stories high, and is constructed of concrete and cement brick. We have been fortunate enough to find several deposits of sand of excellent quality on the farm, and this, combined with the natural gravel foundation has given us very desirable and lasting building material.

Even with these favorable conditions the building has cost about one thousand dollars. The building extends east and west with the coops and runs on the south side. At the left of the entrance at the east end are the stairs leading to the second floorand to the pit for the heater to warm the building. The main floor is about two feet below grade in order to bring the floor level of the coops at a convenient working height and at the same time to keep them level with the ground outside. A four feet passage runs the entire length of the building, on the north side of which there is a concrete shelf arranged to accommodate the hatchers, and of such dimensions that students may operate machines without interfering with each other. On the south side the coops are arranged in pairs with four feet side passages between so as to allow two persons to work in the same passage on opposite sides at the same time. The coops are three by six feet each in floor area, and two and a half feet high. The front of each coop is in two sections, the upper one, twenty inches, is a screen and hinged at the top to swing in backward out of the way, and the lower one, a board ten inches wide, which is stationary, to confine the little chicks and to keep the litter from being scattered outside. The coops are made this height in order to confine a pen of grown fowls when desirable for experiment, demonstration, or to study fancy points. The floors of the coops are of wood, and under this coop floor there is arranged a row of drawers for feed and appliances., This arrangement will serve to keep every thing connected with each pen from becoming separated, or from being misplaced which will be a great convenience to those taking charge of the different lots of chicks. The windows in front of the coops are made to slide up and down, and the upper part of the top half is fitted with a muslin screen, the lower portion being raised when it is desired to give the chicks access to the runs. This arrangement affords an abundance of light as well as ventilation. The outside runs are three feet wide by five and a half feet long, with the sides made of concrete. The fronts are fitted with muslin screens

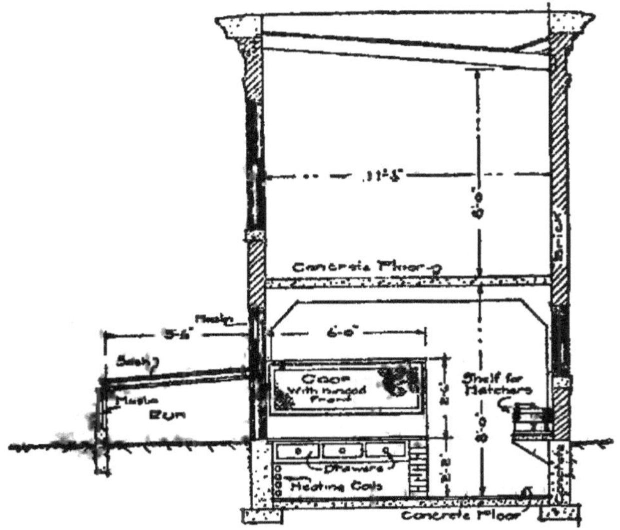

Section of the Hatcher and Brooder House

and over the top are hinged sash somewhat similar to those used in hot beds. The runs are filled with finely sifted earth, and oats will be spaded in to afford green feed in the chicks' scratching ground. While sprouted oats themselves are somewhat large for chicks to handle, the chicks devour the tender shoots which is excellent food for them, and are greatly relished causing them to dig actively, once they have acquired a taste for them. Along the inner wall on the south side under the coops are placed the heating coils for warming the building, and it is intended to maintain a constant temperature of 75 degrees during cold weather. The chicks will be kept in fireless brooders, which, combined with the thorough ventilation, will give outside conditions as nearly as possible without the likelihood of the chicks staying outside too long and becoming chilled.

Running water is provided for the entire house, with a faucet for each pair of pens.

The second floor is used for storage, and also as a feed room for the various grains in bulk that are used for feeding the little chickens and grown fowls. The floor is made of reinforced concrete, thus practically fire-proofing the lower portion of the building.

Altogether it has been our aim so to plan the structure that it will amply serve for school purposes, giving sufficient room to move about without undue interference, and at the same time providing suitable and safe quarters for the hatching apparatus and baby chicks.

OUR NEW SCHOOL AND OFFICE BUILDING.

For the further improvement of our poultry work, and o give better opportunities for those who wish to devote some time with us as students, we have constructed a large building three storeis high, with about 27,000 square feet of floor space. This will give ample facilities for all the work connected with our poultry school including the two departments, the actual doing of all kinds of poultry work under competent instructors, and also for conducting the important branch of our Correspondence School.

This new building is equipped with every modern convenience and device, and will be an ideal place for our work and we shall be very glad to welcome friends and visitors, and give them an actual demonstration of the practical workings of the Philo System.

We know that it is entirely feasible for parties to start a poultry plant of their own with only the Philo System Book as their guide, as thousands of people have done so.

But there are people who wish to begin on an extensive scale who would like to qualify themselves for such an undertaking by getting some practical knowledge at first hand; and for the benefit of such parties we have been furnishing personal instruction for more than a year to persons who have come to Elmira for that purpose. They have been given an opportunity to learn how to do every part of the work of poultry raising, by actually doing the work under competent supervision, and after two or three months' stay they have gone away satisfied with the results, and have started plants of their own or have accepted positions as superintendents of plants for other people.

But there are so many people who cannot spare the time to come here for study, who want further and definite instruction to fit them for successful poultry business that we have determined to establish a Correspondence Course, covering all the theoretical and practical knowledge of the business, dividing the field into ten sections, with a carefully prepared text-book for each, with all the facilities for mastering these lessons that are afforded by the best of the correspondence schools of the country. After each set of lessons has been thoroughly studied, examination questions will be furnished, and these when properly answered will be the basis for a certificate of proficiency with the percentage of accuracy stated.

When one section of the course is finished, the next will come in regular order, and so on until the entire course is completed. Further particulars concerning either branch of our school work will be furnished upon application.

Address
Philo National Poultry Institute,
Elmira, N. Y.

NOTICE

All appliances used in connection with the Philo System can be purchased of the Cycle Hatcher Co., Elmira, N. Y.

Catalogue free.

Complete Index to the Philo System

Coop Construction

Egg Production

Eggs When Prices are High

Fertility

Food

More books from New York History Review

A Short and Sweet History of the Chemung Valley

The Park Church Souvenir Cookbook of 1906

The Great Inter-State Fair

Zim's Foolish History of Elmira

Zim's Foolish History of Horseheads

Frederick Douglass' Speech at Elmira

In Their Honor

In Dairyland

The True Stories series

A Brief History of Chemung County

Cartoons and Caricatures

Our Own Book

The Elmira Prison Camp